Airborne carpet:
Operation Market Garden

Airborne Carpet: Operation Market Garden

Brigadier Anthony Farrar-Hockley DSO MBE MC

Editor-in-Chief: Barrie Pitt
Art Director: Peter Dunbar

Military Consultant: Sir Basil Liddell Hart
Picture Editor: Robert Hunt

Executive Editor: David Mason
Art Editor: Sarah Kingham
Designer: John Marsh
Cover: Denis Piper
Research Assistant: Yvonne Marsh
Cartographer: Richard Natkiel
Special Drawings: John Batchelor

Photographs for this book were especially selected from the following Archives: from left to right page 2-3 Imperial War Museum; 7 IWM; 9 Bundesarchiv; 10 Bundesarchiv; 11 Ullstein; 13 IWM; 16 IWM; 18-19 IWM; 18 IWM; 19 IWM; 20-21 IWM; 23 IWM; 24 IWM; 25 IWM; 27 IWM; 29 IWM; 30-31 IWM; 32 US Army; 33 IWM/Keystone; 35 IWM; 37 IWM; 39 IWM; 40 IWM; 42-43 IWM; 44 IWM; 46 IWM; 47 IWM; 48-49 IWM; 53 Ullstein; 54-55 IWM; 56 Ullstein/Suddeutscher Verlag; 57 Ullstein; 58-59 IWM; 60 Bibliothek fur Zeitgeschichte; 62 Ullstein; 66-67 Ullstein; 73 US Army; 74-75 IWM; 76 US Army; 77 IWM; 79 IWM; 80 IWM; 81 IWM; 82-83 IWM; 84 IWM; 85 IWM; 88 IWM; 89 US Army; 91 IWM; 94 US Army; 95 US Army; 96 US Army; 97 IWM; 99 IWM; 101 US Army; 103 IWM; 104-105 IWM; 108-109 IWM; 109 IWM; 111 Ullstein; 113 Sudd. Verlag; 114 Ullstein/IWM; 115 Sudd. Verlag; 116-117 US Army; 118 IWM; 119 IWM; 120-121 IWM; 120 IWM; 125 IWM; 128-129 IWM; 129 US Army; 130-131 IWM; 132 IWM; 133 IWM; 136 IWM; /IWM; 137 IWM; 139 Sudd. Verlag; 140/141 IWM; 141 Ullstein; 142-143 IWM; 144 IWM; 149 Ullstein; 151 IWM; 156-157 Ullstein; 157 Ullstein; 159 Ullstein.

Copyright © 1969
by Anthony Farrar-Hockley

First published in the United States of America.
This edition first published in Great Britain
in 1970 by Macdonald & Co. (Publishers) Ltd.,
49 Poland Street, London W1

PRINTED IN FINLAND

Contents

8 Crises and tensions
26 Brereton's army
36 The plan is made
52 'Whence this strange intelligence?'
68 16th September
72 Market begins
102 Garden opens
110 Monday, 18th September
124 The struggle for Hell's Highway
148 'Boys, it is all hell'
160 Bibliography

The thrust to cross the Rhine

Introduction by Captain Sir Basil Liddell Hart

The German rally after the Allied break-out from Normandy at the end of August 1944 was much helped by the Allies' supply difficulties, which reduced the first onset to a lightweight charge that could be checked by a hastily improvised defence, and then curtailed the build-up of the Allied armies for a powerful attack. In part, the supply difficulties were due to the length of the Allies' own advance. In part, they were due to the Germans' strategy in leaving garrisons behind to hold the French ports. The fact that the Allies were thus denied the use of Dunkirk, Calais, Boulogne and le Havre, as well as the big ports in Brittany, became a powerful indirect brake on the Allies' offensive. Although they had captured the still greater port of Antwerp in good condition, the enemy kept a tenacious grip on the estuary of the Schelde, and thus prevented the Allies making use of the port.

Before the break-out from Normandy, their supplies had to be carried less than twenty miles from the base in order to replenish the striking forces. They now had to be carried nearly 300 miles. The burden was thrown almost entirely on the Allies' motor transport, as the French railway network had been destroyed by previous air attacks.

In mid-September a bold attempt was made to loosen the stiffening resistance by dropping three airborne divisions behind the German right flank in Holland, to clear the way for a fresh drive by the British Second Army up to and over the Lower Rhine. By dropping the airborne forces in successive layers over a sixty-mile belt of country behind the German front a foothold was gained on all four of the strategic stepping-stones needed to cross the interval – the passage of the Wilhelmina Canal at Eindhoven, of the Maas (Meuse) at Grave, of the Waal and Lek (the two branches of the Rhine) at Nijmegen and Arnhem respectively. Three of these four stepping-stones were secured and passed. But a stumble at the third forfeited the chance of securing the fourth, in face of the Germans' speedy reaction.

This check led to the frustration of the overland thrust and the sacrifice of the 1st Airborne Division at Arnhem. But the possibility of outflanking the Rhine defence-line was a strategic prize that justified the stake and the exceptional boldness of dropping airborne forces so far behind the front. The 1st Airborne Division maintained its isolated position at Arnhem for ten days instead of the two that were reckoned as the maximum to be expected. But the chances of success were lessened by the way that the descent of the airborne forces at these four successive points, in a straight line, sign-posted all too clearly the direction of the Second Army's thrust.

The obviousness of the aim simplified the opponent's problem in concentrating his available reserves to hold the final stepping-stone, and to overthrow the British airborne forces there, before the leading troops of the Second Army arrived to relieve them. The nature of the Dutch countryside, with its 'canalized' routes, also helped the defenders in obstructing the advance, while there was a lack of wider moves to mask the directness of the approach and to distract the defender.

After the failure of the Arnhem gamble, the prospect of early victory faded. The Allies were thrown back on the necessity of building up their resources along the frontiers of Germany for a massive offensive of a deliberate kind. The build-up was bound to take time, but the Allied Command increased its own handicap by concentrating, first, on an attempt to force the Aachen gateway into Germany, rather than on clearing the shores of the Scheldt to open up a fresh supply route. The American advance on Aachen developed into a too direct approach, and its progress was repeatedly checked.

Along the rest of the Western Front the efforts of the Allied armies during September and October 1944 amounted to little more than a process of nibbling. Meantime the German defence was being continuously reinforced – with such reserves as could be scraped from elsewhere, and with freshly raised forces, beyond the troops which had managed to make their way back from France. The German build-up along the front was progressing faster than that of the Allies, despite Germany's great inferiority of material resources. The Schelde Estuary was not cleared of the enemy until early in November.

The account of this great airborne operation, the most dramatic in the later stages of the war, has been written for this series by one of the men best qualified to deal with it, Brigadier Anthony Farrar-Hockley, himself an exceptionally experienced and distinguished parachute commander. His story is wonderfully detailed, while remarkably vivid, and forms one of the most outstanding books in the whole series.

Crises and tensions

On the night 18th/19th August 1944, Field-Marshal Günther von Kluge committed suicide by taking poison as he travelled out of France towards Germany.

It was a mean end to a man who had held many posts of high responsibility. That summer, he had succeeded Field-Marshal von Rundstedt as commander-in-chief of all German forces in the west: Army Group B, commanded by the intrepid Rommel, struggling to stem the influx of the allied invasion in Normandy; Eberbach's Panzer Group West, fighting with them; Army Group G under Blaskowitz – nine divisions in southern France watching the Mediterranean shore; the lines of communication to them through the Low Countries and France; and the forward bases.

Rundstedt had been relieved of this enormous command because he had failed to throw back the American and British assault forces into the Channel waters. The old Field-Marshal was tired; exasperated by Hitler's continual interference in the day-to-day conduct of battle. As in Russia, so in France, a division or higher could not be moved without the Führer's agreement. Precise instructions were sent down to the commander-in-chief for counterattacks detailing strength, direction and timing. When one of these had failed at the end of June with the loss of a considerable number of tanks, Rundstedt was asked by a member of Hitler's staff what should be done next.

'Make peace, you fools,' the Field-Marshal shouted into the telephone. 'What else can you do?'

Kluge was at that moment with Hitler. Recently recovered from a motor accident on the Russian front, he had been ordered to attend the Supreme Headquarters prior to taking up a new post, for a personal briefing on the war situation by the Führer. Rundstedt's advice to make peace was quoted to him as an example of the 'defeatism' which inhibited German arms in Normandy.

'Now you are to be commander-in-chief in the west,' he was told. 'And you see what it is that needs to be put right.'

An artillery officer in origin, the new commander-in-chief was a man of

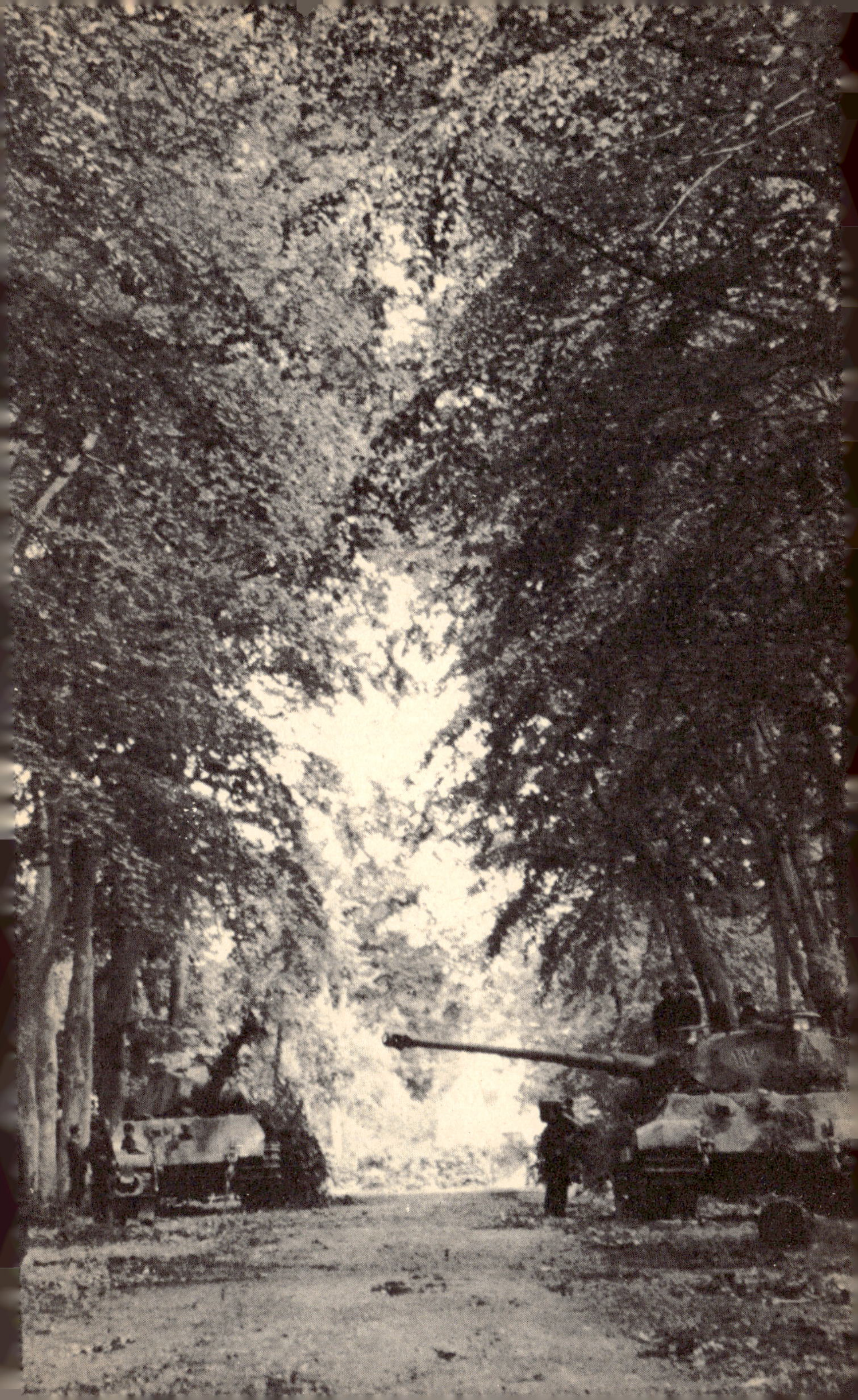

Above: Field-Marshal von Runstedt (right) poses while visiting troops as Commander-in-Chief, west. *Below:* Field-Marshal von Kluge (centre) inspecting defences in France, July, 1944. *Right:* Field-Marshal Model surveying defences, 11th September, 1944

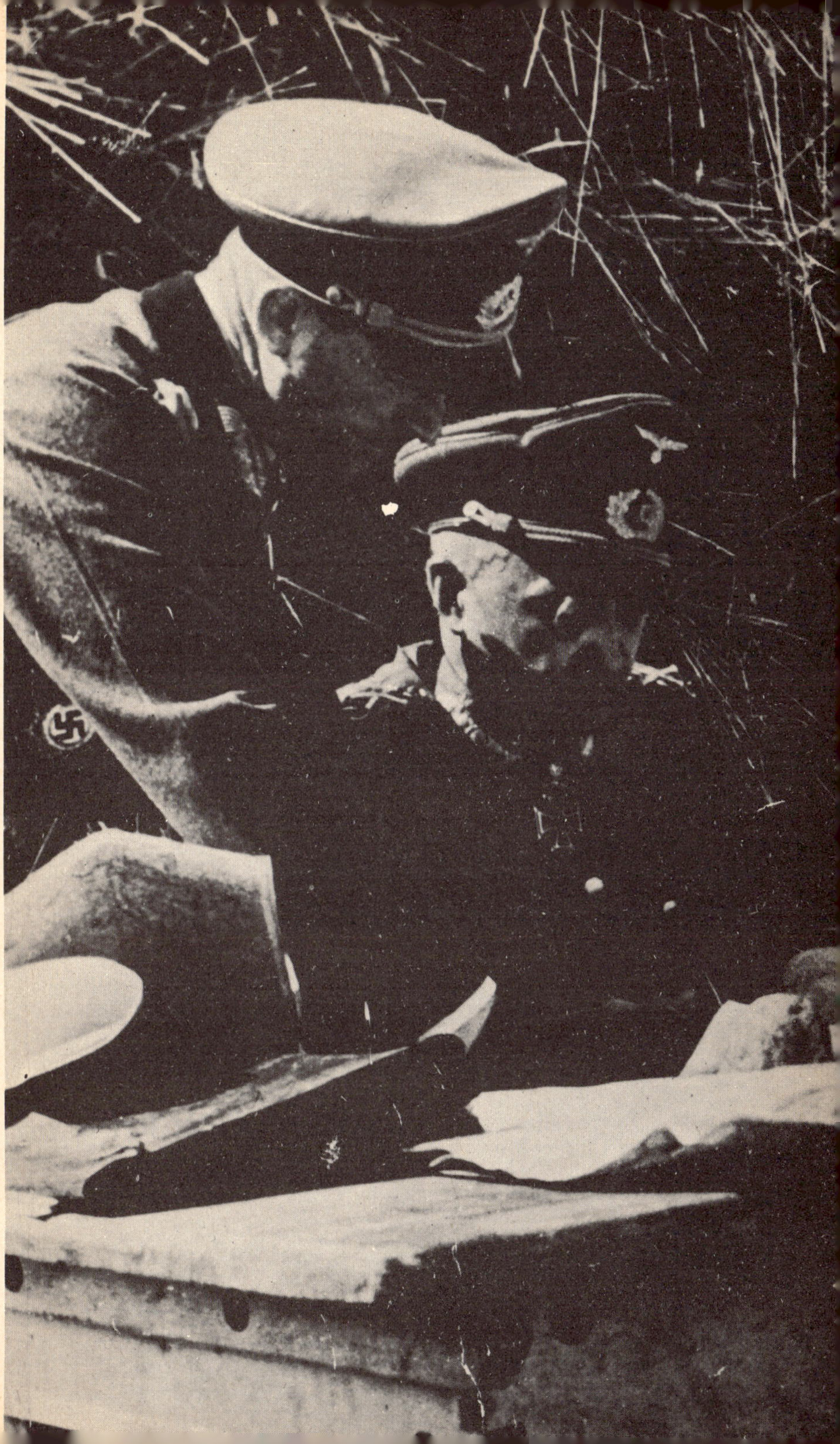

quick intelligence but lacking in warmth. His soldiers called him 'clever Hans'. On arrival in France he spoke sharply to the subordinates awaiting him, this open criticism leading to a quarrel with Rommel. Within a few days, however, a tour of his command showed him that he must apologise to his staff and army group commanders. Not only was there no chance of defeating the invasion force; the German contestants would shortly themselves be defeated piecemeal unless several divisions at least were drawn back. While Kluge was trying to convince Hitler that such moves were necessary, Rommel was wounded. Kluge was obliged to go forward to the headquarters of Army Group B at La Roche Guyon, on the Seine, to take personal command.

He was now somewhat absorbed in the handling of a battle subject increasingly to the enemy's initiative. Then suddenly, on 20th July, there came news of an altogether different kind: an attempt had been made on Hitler's life. Kluge's attention was diverted from the fighting at the front by this sensational event within Germany. Like many of his senior colleagues, he had been aware that a coup was in the wind but was not a conspirator. For some hours, no one in the west knew whether Hitler was dead or alive. There followed an urgent signal from Supreme Headquarters asserting that the Führer had survived and was to broadcast to the nation. 'Clever Hans' acted in character. He declined to support the conspiracy, to bring over the forces in the west in open revolution. Equally, he made no attempt to arrest those principals in the plot, now revealed to him, in his command. He simply returned to the direction of the battle.

There was ample work here to occupy his whole attention. On 1st August, American forces at Avranches broke through the German defence ring. General Patton's Third Army began to race away south and then east while the Canadians, British and part of an American army steadily ground down the concentration of German forces immediately south of Caen. Kluge hurried to the front and could not be contacted. Hitler took fright, suspecting that he had gone to negotiate an armistice secretly and inclined to the view that this was connected with the attempted assassination. Disenchanted with Field-Marshal von Kluge, he directed him to return to Germany without explanation or warning.

Having written a reproachful letter to the Führer, Kluge left La Roche Guyon and set off in his motor car, ostensibly for Germany, in fact to a suicide's end near Metz.

In the six and a half weeks that he had held command in the west, his forces had dwindled alarmingly; half the German soldiers in Normandy and Brittany had been killed, wounded or captured and two thirds of their armour, artillery and transport lost. Attempts had been made by the air force to support him on the ground and relieve his divisions from air attack. All such operations had failed. Once, there was a hope of effective intervention when 300 day fighters were assembled to strike from Luftwaffe airfields in France. None reached the battle area. The Allied air forces controlled the skies.

In such a situation, Kluge's successor, Field-Marshal Walther Model, took up his post.

Despite an eyeglass and scarred cheeks, Model was neither a Prussian, *hochwohlgeboren*, nor in any other sense of heritage a pattern of the officer corps. Uncouth, given to deriding officers in front of their men, he had been helped to high rank due to his allegiance to Hitler and the National Socialist Party. But there had been other talents to recommend him: courage in battle amply demonstrated in two world wars; a quick tactical brain and a power of ruthless command; a restless energy. He knew well that Hitler had no doubts as to his loyalty and admired the dogged skill with which he had conducted several hazardous defensive battles with the Russians. On the several public occasions when the Führer had attempted to bully him, he had staunchly resisted with the rough manners he used to everyone. Thus, while he now declined to discuss Hitler's handling of the war with the chiefs-of-staff at Headquarters, West and Army Group B, he was equally

Lieutenant-General George S Patton

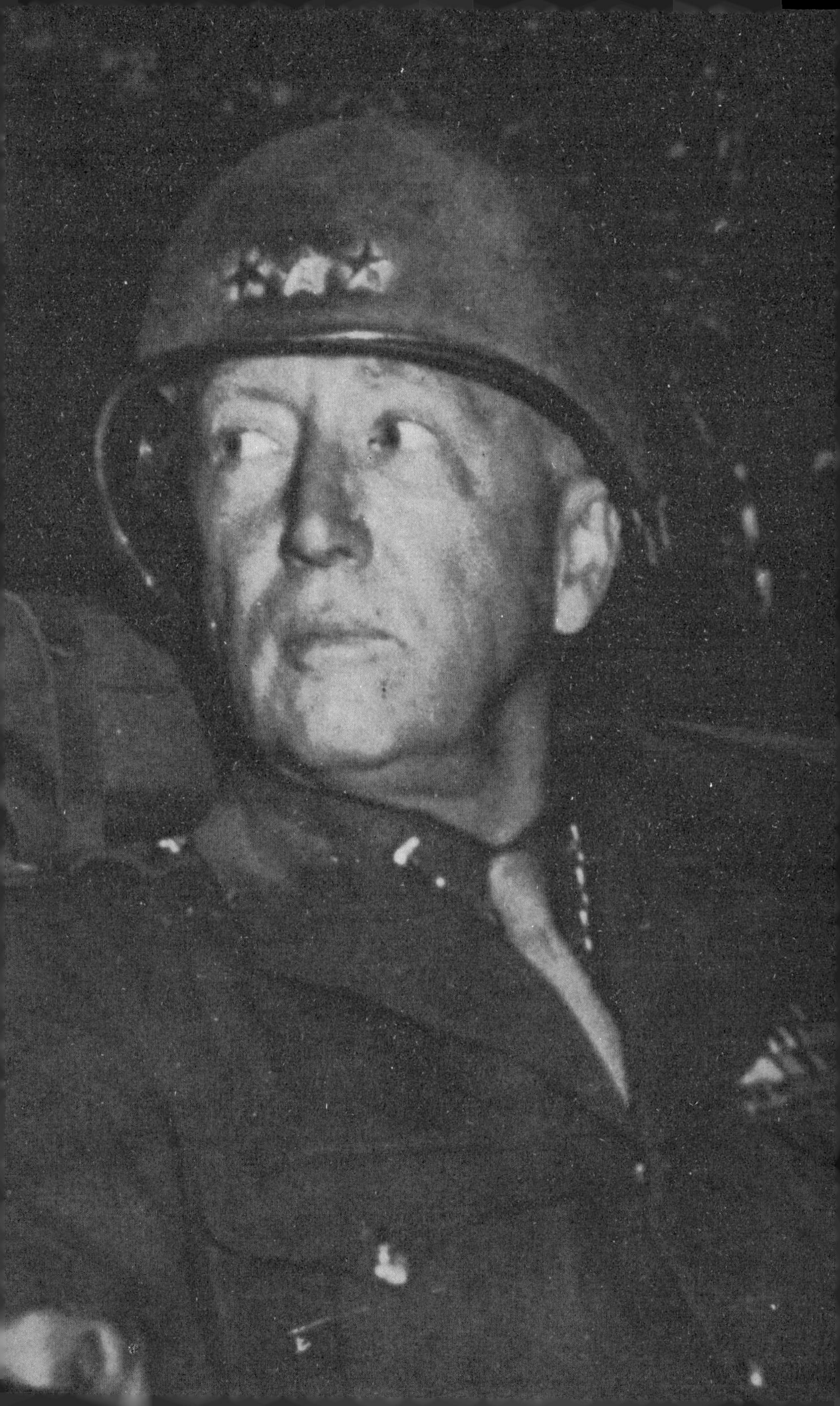

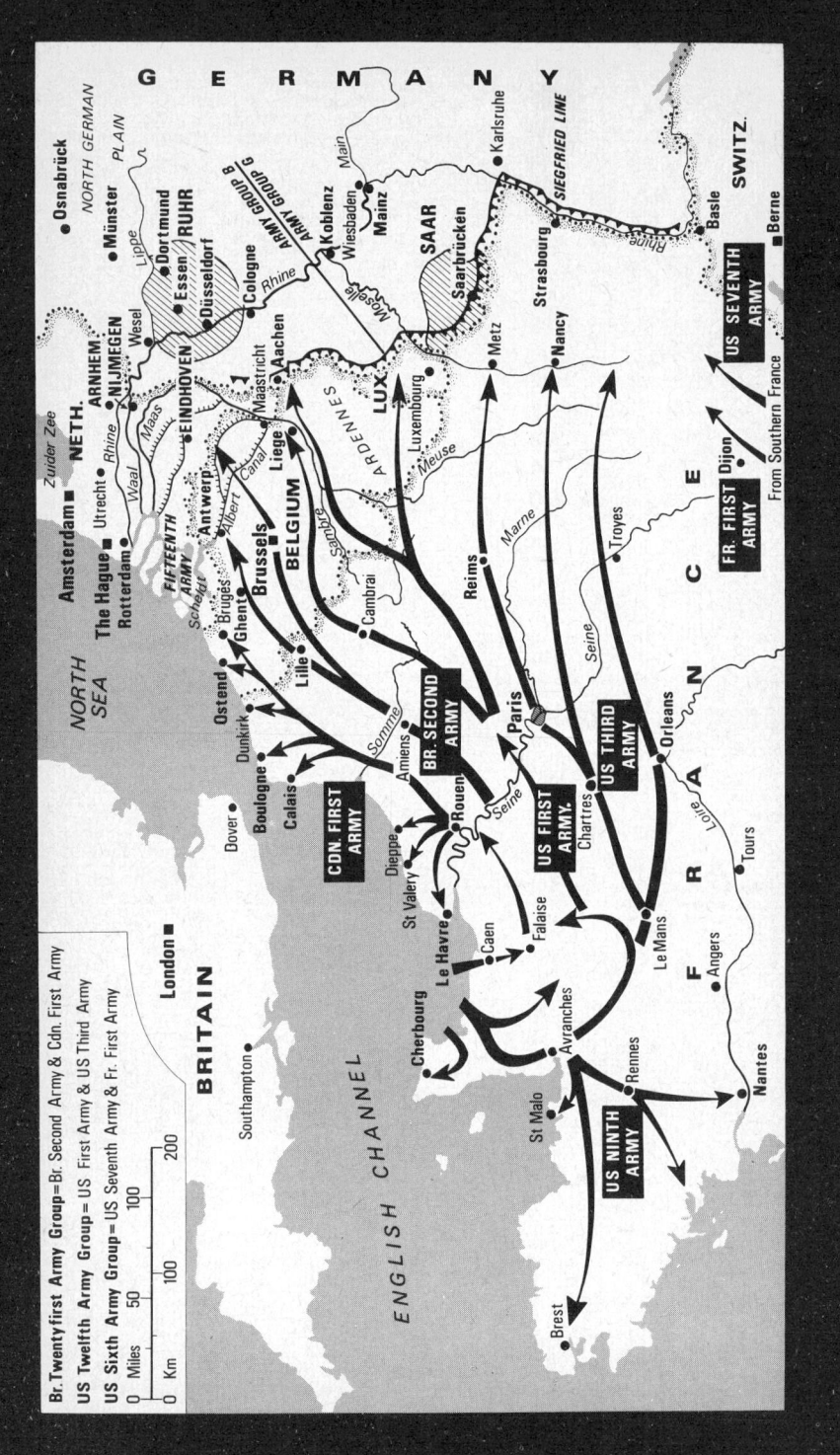

The Allied advances: Patton's American 3rd, Hodge's American 1st, Dempsey's 2nd British and Crerar's 1st Canadian armies

unprepared to accept orders from the Führer or his staff which endangered his command.

It was fortunate for the Germans that Model had arrived. Within a few days, the consequences of the American break-out were alarming. The second American army was soon swelling the flood tide streaming eastward.

Next, the British and Canadians, having destroyed the large group of divisions left forward at Hitler's insistence, were able to begin a rapid advance of their own; while from southern France, Army Group G fell back with difficulty as an allied invasion force pushed north from the Mediterranean sea. On 24th August, Model told Supreme Headquarters that he needed '. . . at least thirty to thirty-five infantry divisions, and twelve Panzer divisions.' It was already clear that a stand on the river Seine could not be made. 'We must look ahead and build more rearward positions behind the Somme-Marne line up to and including the West Wall (on the German border).' At midnight on the 29th, his summary of operations for the day included this assessment: 'the eleven Panzer and Panzer Grenadier divisions have only five to ten tanks each.' From these he might form eleven battle groups each of a tank company, armoured infantry battalion, reconnaissance and supporting troops; but even this would not be possible unless there were replacements of men and armour. He could also form four infantry divisions out of the sixteen which had, in one condition or another, reached the Seine. But these men '. . . have only a few heavy weapons and for the most part are equipped with nothing more than small arms. . . . There is no reserve whatever of assault guns and other heavy anti-tank equipment.'

The ingenious work of Albert Speer, *Reishsminister* for armament and war production, contrived to supply some of the deficiencies in armour and guns. There were adequate stocks of ammunition for the services but supplies of petrol were declining. There were, of course, no fresh divisions available; and the reinforcement depots had long since been stripped of every man fit to fight. Recourse was had to the young and the old, the age limit dropping to fifteen and rising to sixty, a measure which brought just over 500,000 recruits into the army. Many of these youths and men were put into twenty-five new *Volkskammer* divisions to bolster the local defence of the towns and villages of the Reich. For Hitler and his immediate entourage, political and military, saw now what the commanders in the field had seen long since: the British and Americans and French were approaching the frontiers of the homeland.

The propaganda machine began its work of warning. Rundstedt, re-appointed commander-in-chief in the west on 5th September, issued an order of the day:

'Soldiers Of The Western Front! I expect you to defend Germany's sacred soil to the very last!'

Model, at Army Group B, demanded:

'Soldiers! None of us gives up a square foot of German soil while still alive. . . . Whoever retreats without giving battle is a traitor to his people.'

In less heroic terms, Himmler, chief of the Gestapo, had the following notice issued on 10th September:

'Certain unreliable elements seem to believe that the war will be over for them as soon as they surrender to the enemy.

'Against this belief it must be pointed out that every deserter will be prosecuted and will find his just punishment. Furthermore, his ignominious behaviour will entail the most severe consequences for his family – they will be summarily shot.'

Having survived a bomb explosion at his feet and having armies still in being and a proportion of supplies to meet their needs, Hitler still hoped to save Germany from invasion and total defeat. Briefing two new chiefs of staff for Headquarters West and Army Group B on 31st August he remarked: '. . . at a time of heavy military defeats it is quite childish and naïve to look for a politically favourable moment to make a move. . . . The time will come when the tension between the allies becomes so strong that, in spite of everything, the rupture occurs. History teaches us that all coalitions break up, but you must await the moment however difficult the waiting may be. I intend to con-

Above: General Eisenhower, Supreme Commander, and the US Navy Secretary, James V Forrestal. *Below:* Lieutenant-General Hodges, General Montgomery, Lieutenant-Generals Bradley and Dempsey after a meeting at Headquarters, 21st Army Group

tinue fighting until there is a possibility of a decent peace which is bearable for Germany and secures the life of future generations. Then I shall make it. Whatever happens, we shall carry on this struggle until, as Frederick the Great said, "one of our damned enemies gives up in despair".'

The tensions between the allies were somewhat less than Hitler anticipated. He failed to understand how united they were in determination to destroy his dictatorship and hence ready to resolve their differences.

Nonetheless, as the break-out from the beach-head began to show promise of becoming an overwhelming success, tensions hitherto absent during the perilous period of landing and lodgement were manifested. They arose in two interconnected matters: personality and strategy.

The personality of General Montgomery had been accepted, grudgingly or otherwise, during planning and landing. General Eisenhower, as supreme commander, had appointed this experienced and confident British leader as co-ordinator of all the ground forces for the invasion phase. Thereafter, it had been made clear, as soon as SHAEF, Supreme Headquarters of the Allied Expeditionary Force, was established in France, Eisenhower would become his own commander-in-chief of ground forces, controlling directly the Canadian/British army group under Montgomery and an American army group under General Omar Bradley.

Eisenhower expected that, as the beach-head filled with fighting divisions, the area held by the allies would expand to a major lodgement, extending west to Brittany and its deep water ports and harbours and north-east to the Seine, which some optimistically hoped they might reach by the first week in September. There would then be a pause while the newly opened ports and harbours received reinforcements of men and material, while railways were restored and airfields cleared and while the administrative base was made ready with forward dumps and transport companies to support the next offensive which should carry the allied line to the German frontier by May 1945. But as Clausewitz tells us, no plan survives the first contact of war.

By mid-August, less than ten weeks after the landings, Montgomery's generalship and Hitler's fanatical determination to defend the Normandy *bocage* bank by bank had clearly combined to produce a very different situation to that envisaged in the secret planning rooms in London. The prime strength of the Nazi armies in France was being ground to destruction in the Falaise pocket; Patton's army had begun its run towards the Seine. The clearance of Brittany had become a minor operation to be completed at their leisure·

On 17th August, Montgomery put it to Bradley that a new strategy was needed; both because the break-out was taking place much earlier than they had originally expected and because it was being conducted in very different circumstances: the Germans' capability seriously to resist further in France had been smashed. The advantage was theirs. His own Army Group (21st) and Bradley's (12th) should combine 'after crossing the Seine together as a solid mass of forty divisions, which would be so strong that it need fear nothing. This force should advance northwards, passing through Belgium north of the Ardennes and then directly into Germany, through the Ruhr and across the flat German plain, depriving Hitler of all his centres of war production.

Now the tensions began to appear.

Bradley appeared to concur with this idea; but it was clear to him that its adoption would mean that he remained under Montgomery's command, however loosely. He was not a petty-minded man but there were influences other than his own patriotic inclination to persuade him that American troops should be under a wholly American command. Already, the error of a press censor at SHAEF had exacerbated the question of command:

'*New York Herald Tribune:* SHAEF, August 16th. The top press relations officer at General Dwight D. Eisenhower's supreme headquarters had the embarrassing duty early today of denying a major story that had been previously corroborated and passed by SHAEF's own military censors, and already had front-page prominence in

Above: Part of the host of prisoners taken during the break-out of the Allies from Normandy, August, 1944. *Below:* An example of the widespread destruction of German vehicles and equipment during the break-out. *Below right:* Infantry of the British 43rd (Wessex) Division crossing the Seine, 25th August, 1944

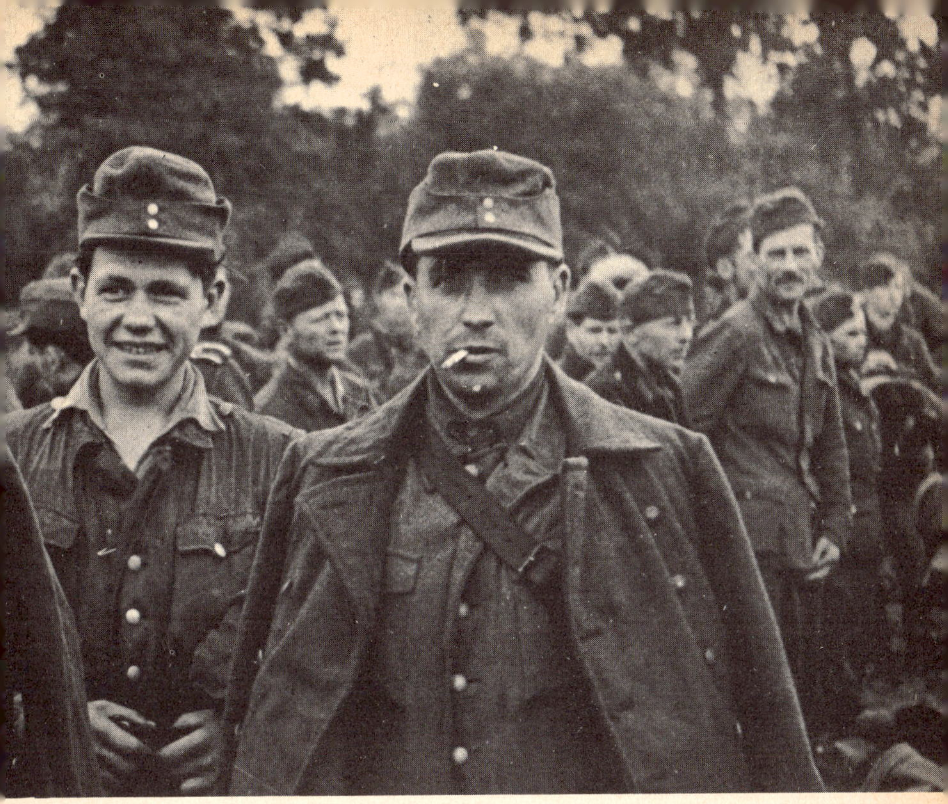

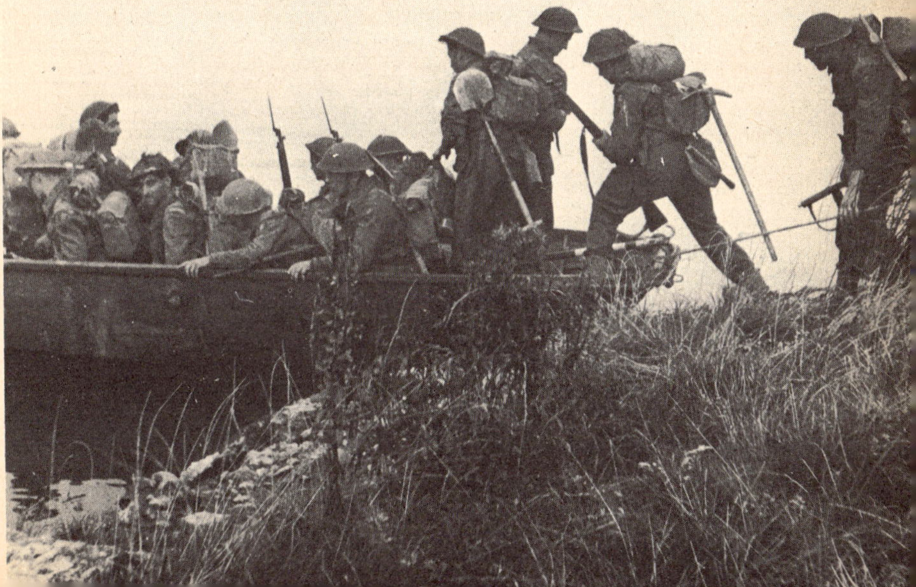

Royal Engineers bridge the Seine

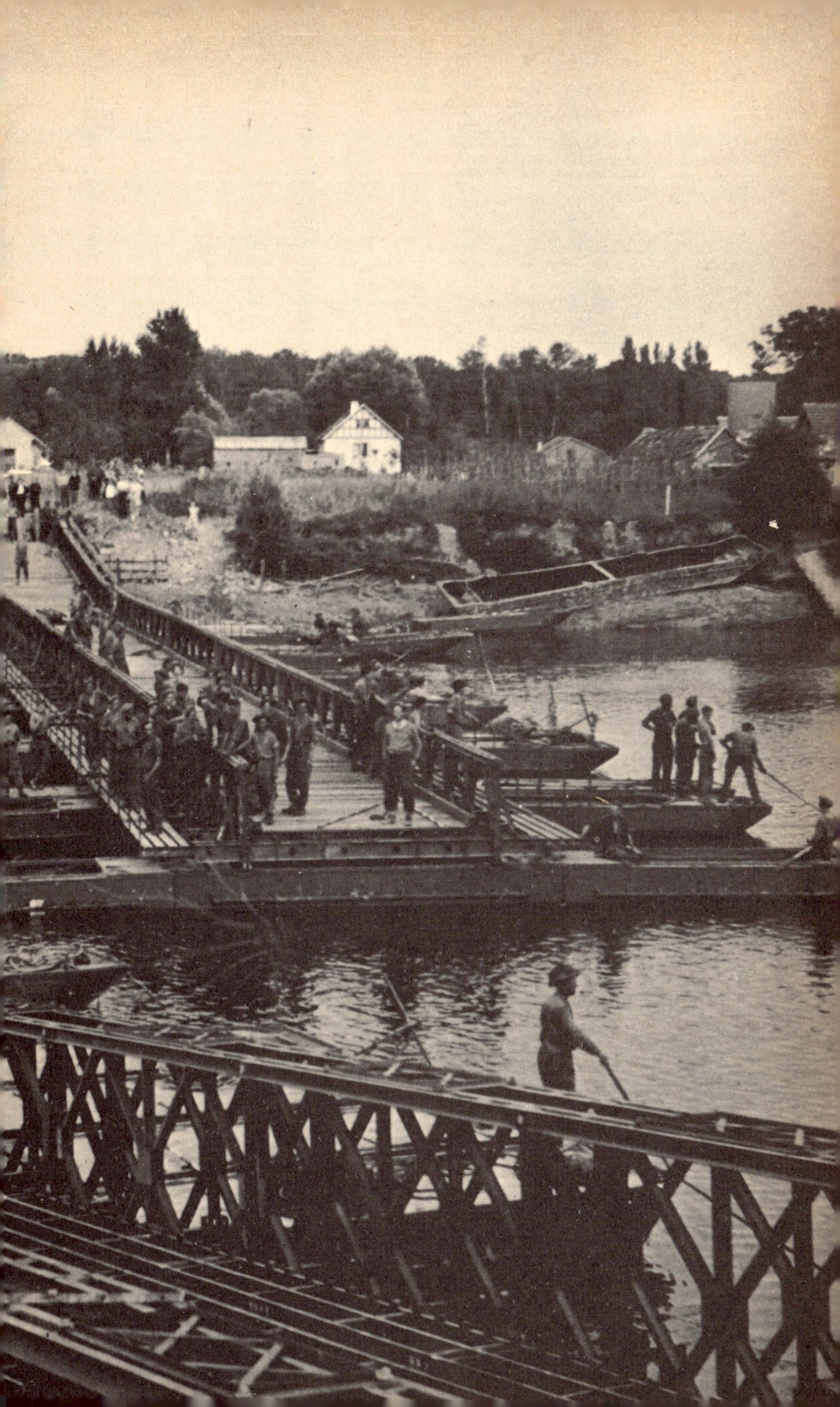

the first editions of all London's papers....

'The story, so officially and flatly denied, was that General Eisenhower had taken over the active direction of the Allied forces in Normandy and Brittany, that General Sir Bernard L Montgomery remained in command of the 21st Army Group, which includes British, Canadian and Polish troops, and that General Omar N Bradley had been given an equal status with General Montgomery in command of the 12th Army Group which includes the 1st and 3rd American armies and the 2nd French Division.

'The official version at this moment of writing, 0106 hours, double British summer time, 16th August, is that General Eisenhower is in France in "active command", that a 12th army group has been set up under General Bradley, as reported, but that General Montgomery, in addition to being in command of the 21st Army Group, also is the top-ranking ground commander of the invasion forces, still outranking General Bradley, who remains subordinate to him.'

The native pride of Britain expressed a different view in the London Daily Mirror next day:

'We feel it our duty to demand that General Montgomery be given an apology... The meaning (of the SHAEF release) seemed plain. Montgomery had been demoted, and that is the meaning which hundreds of thousands of people must have attached to the statement.'

General Marshall wrote from Washington to Eisenhower to say that both he and the Secretary for War felt it was time that Bradley should be answerable directly to the supreme commander. 'The late announcement (that Montgomery retained overall command of land forces) I have just referred to has cast a damper on the public enthusiasm.'

Eisenhower replied, 'It seems that so far as the press and public are concerned a resounding victory is not sufficient; the question of "how" is equally important.'

Meantime, Bradley had put forward a different strategy which he and Patton, commander of Third Army, had discussed, and which they considered would permit a surer and quicker way of pushing allied troops into Germany. Taking the shortest route, the Rhine should be crossed between Wiesbaden and Karlsruhe and a thrust developed north-east along the Main valley. Patton believed that he could do this with his own army, though neither he nor Bradley explained how they would fight their way alone through the densely-wooded hills beyond the source of the Main.

All this Eisenhower mulled over before he held a conference, at which Montgomery was present, on 23rd August. It was not easy for the supreme commander to make a decision. Already the chain of supply was becoming strained. Cherbourg was the only major port opening for use and this was 400 miles from Patton's armour crossing the Seine. New railway track was going down faster than they had predicted; the engineers were rebuilding bridges, clearing airfields and opening roads at an exceptional pace. Even so, the forward troops were outstripping the resources of the supply organisation. The four armies moving through France were using about 1,000,000 gallons of motor spirit each day. There were insufficient transport aircraft, railway tracks, or road trucks to carry such a tonnage forward once the Seine was crossed.

Once the Seine was crossed, Paris would be freed and the initial supply of the city would fall upon Eisenhower's supply bases – there was no other organisation to take it on; and there were no means of transporting the supplies except his own aircraft, rail locomotives and trucks.

In addition to these considerations and the furore concerning the command of American soldiers, the supreme commander had been asked by the British government to overrun as soon as possible the bases in the Pas de Calais from which Hitler's V1s – the flying bombs – were being launched on London and the home counties.

The upshot was a compromise, a concession to some of the wishes of both army group commanders together with an implicit policy of wait-and-see. 21st Army Group should clear

Tanks hastening through France en route for Belgium

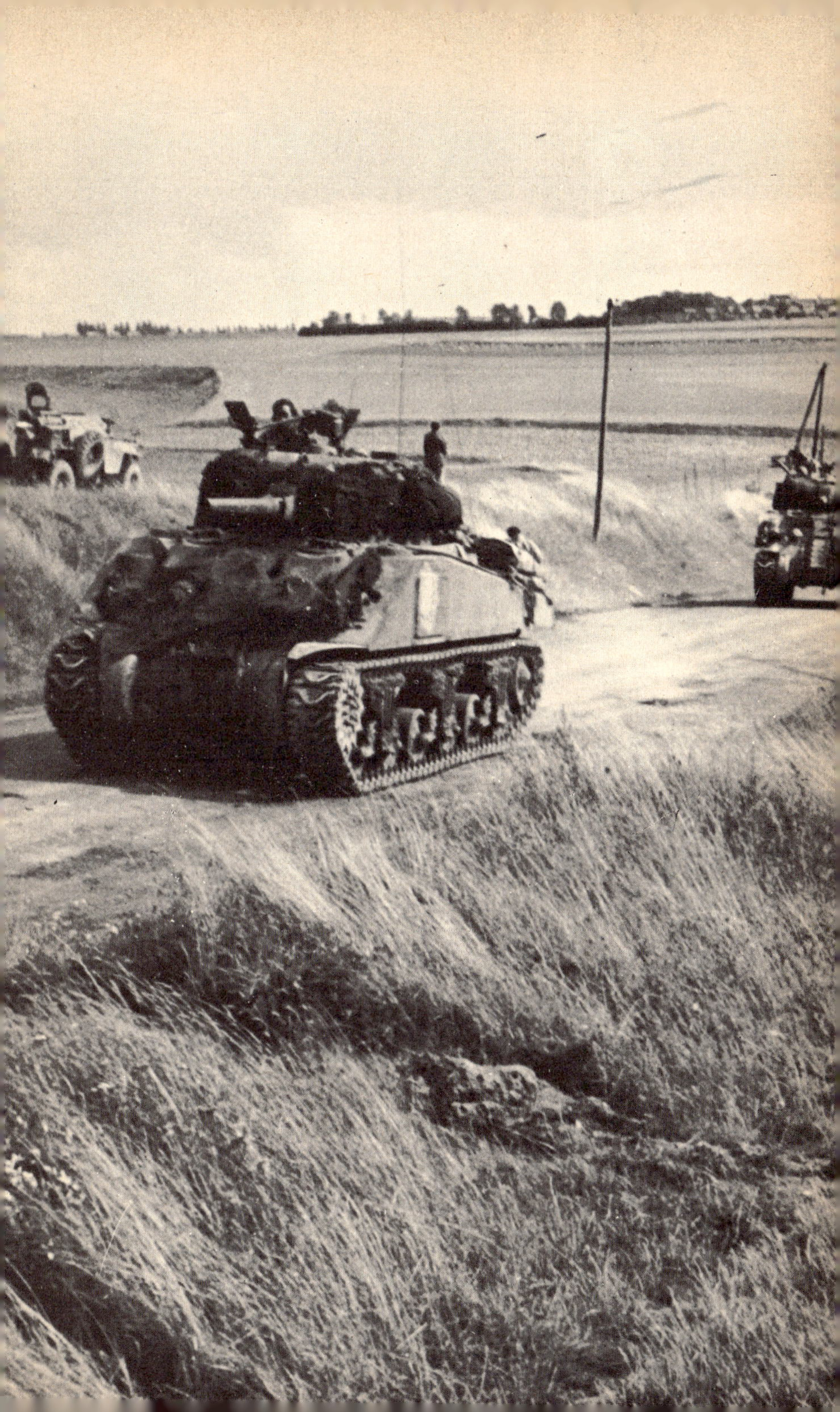

Above: Motor Cyclists pass German truck on the Brussels road. *Above right:* The British enter Brussels

through to Belgium, cleaning out the Pas de Calais and securing the port of Antwerp, while the American First Army guarded its southern flank. Bradley was to prepare to open an offensive south of the Ardennes. The bulk of supplies would go to Montgomery's force and '... All of us having agreed upon this general plan,' Eisenhower wrote to Montgomery, 'the principal thing we must now strive for is speed in execution. All the Supply people have assured us that they can support (your) move, beginning this minute – let us assume that they know exactly what they are talking about and get about it vigorously and without delay.'

So they did.

By 4th September, 21st Army Group had captured Antwerp and Brussels while Patton's Third Army, despite its thin ration of petrol, had crossed the Meuse and was advancing on Metz.

On 1st September, Eisenhower's forward headquarters had opened in France and he had assumed direct command of the two army groups forward. Shortly, he would draw in the 6th Army Group advancing from the Mediterranean shore. All were now aware that the time for wait-and-see was over. A decision as to how the expeditionary force should advance into Germany must no longer be deferred.

At SHAEF, it seemed to Eisenhower that nothing could withhold their continuing advance, other than the limitations of supply. The British and Canadians should drive on to the Ruhr, the Americans to the Saar as he had planned long ago. On 2nd September, meeting Bradley at Chartres with Hodges of the First and Patton of the Third Army in attendance, he gave consent to 12th Army Group extending into Germany. Though all three generals were warned that 21st Army

Group would still have priority in supply, the dashing Patton did not need more than the nod of either Eisenhower or Bradley to press on. He hoped and believed that he would achieve such a success as would necessitate a reversal of supply policy in his favour.

Unfortunately, while Eisenhower recognised the dangers of their circumstances, he does not seem to have recognised that his encouragement of both army groups was to lead to the very loss of initiative against which he warned. His letter to General Marshall on 4th September indicates that, surprisingly, his appreciation had not been taken to its conclusion.

'The closer we get to the Siegfried Line, the more we will be stretched administratively, and eventually a period of relative inaction will be imposed upon us. The potential danger is that while we are temporarily stalled the enemy will be able to pick up bits and pieces of forces everywhere and reorganise them swiftly for defending (their frontier) or the Rhine. It is obvious from an overall viewpoint we must now as never before keep the enemy stretched as never before.'

The stretching of the enemy and the supply line were directly related, however: in attempting to give some sustenance to both army groups, there would be enough for neither, particularly in motor spirit. At the limit of their resources, the diversion of even a fragment of their fuel supplies halted 21st Army Group. What was diverted, Patton soon discovered, was insufficient to sustain his plans to 'git up and go'. To the astonishment of Rundstedt and Model, to the gratification of Hitler, the allied expeditionary force came to a halt at the very moment when the German forces in the west were spent.

From this lost opportunity, out of this circumstance, Operation Market Garden was born.

Brereton's army

In September, 1944, Lieutenant-General Lewis H Brereton was an airman in command of an unusual army. The chief of the United States Ninth Air Force for the Normandy invasion, he was selected by General Eisenhower as the summer progressed to create a new organisation: an army of parachute and glider-borne troops combined with the air squadrons needed to convey them to battle. Departing for a visit to France in July, Eisenhower instructed his chief of staff to leave Brereton in no doubt as to the importance of his post.

'Brereton should be working in his new job instantly. Please inform him that I am particularly anxious about the navigational qualifications of the transport command crews. He is to get on to this in an intensive way and to keep me in touch with his progress. There is nothing we are undertaking about which I am more concerned than this job of his. I want him on the ball with all his might.'

In August, the First Allied Airborne Army came into being.

American and British airborne forces had taken an important part in the Normandy landings and, though scattered, had carried out effectively the tasks they had been given. These tasks achieved, they were returned to the United Kingdom to re-equip so as to be ready for further operations at short notice. But as the break-out battle developed, the airborne soldiers began to feel like the man who took his harp to a party; no one would ask them to play. Brereton, taking command of these eager warriors, found also to his vexation that his ideas for intensified air navigation training—indeed for the joint ground and air training of his whole force—were frustrated as, increasingly, the aircraft were called to France to shuttle supplies to the racing armies.

Brereton's vexation was shared in Washington. General Marshall, Chief-of-Staff of the United States Army, and his air colleague, General 'Hap' Arnold, believed that a valuable weapon in the expeditionary force was being overlooked. Not for the first

**Lieutenant-General Lewis H Brereton
Commander, First Allied
Airborne Army**

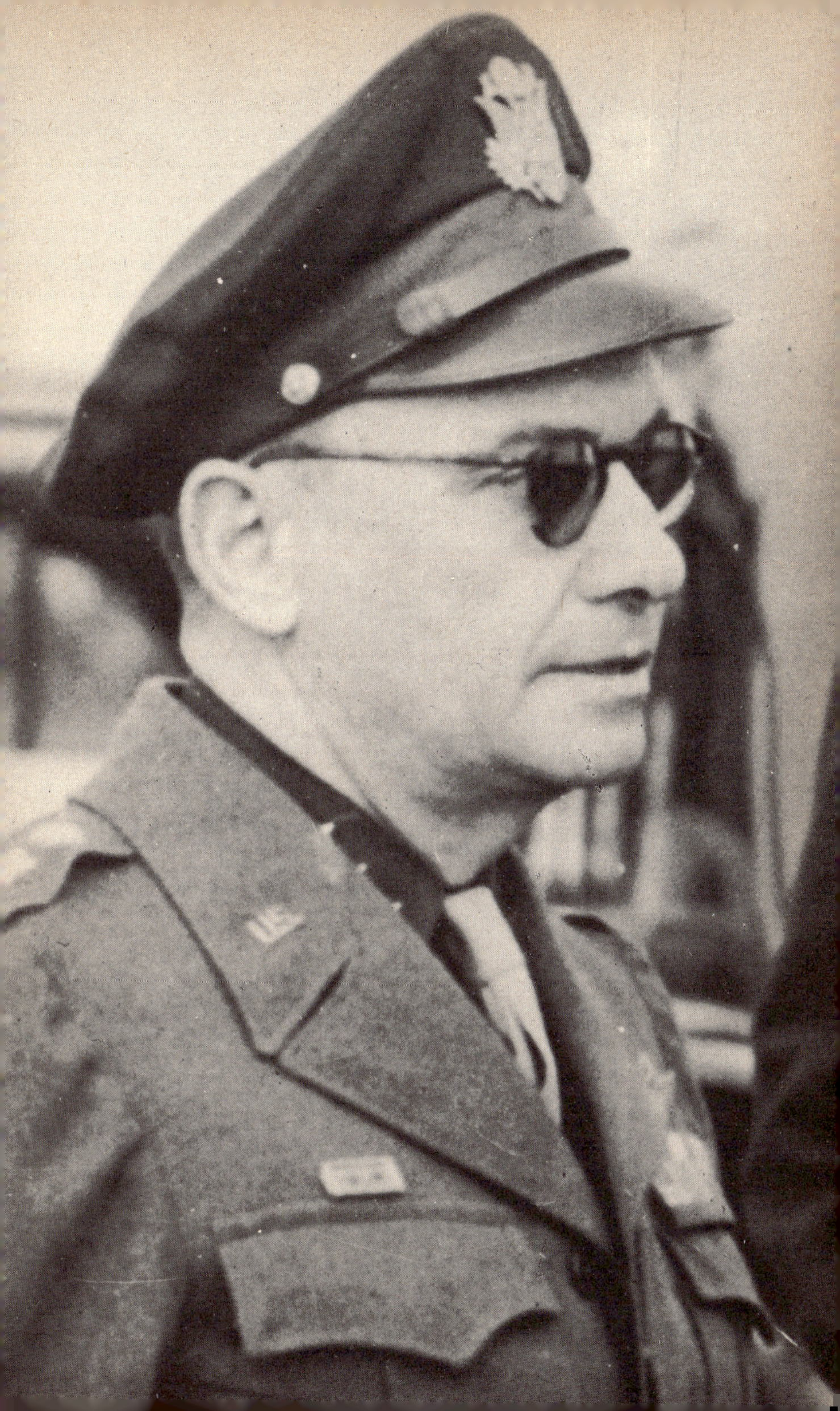

time, they reminded General Eisenhower that it was there.

The supreme commander did not need the reminder. He had already had numerous plans drafted for their use which the speed of advance had nullified. Most of these had been for the benefit of the northern army group but in early September he again offered Brereton's army to Bradley, proposing a mass descent in the Maastricht-Aachen area to assist Hodges' troops through the Siegfried Line. When Bradley replied that he did not want airborne soldiers but preferred to keep their aircraft to 'feed gas to George Patton's (Third Army)', Eisenhower directed Brereton elsewhere. He was 'to operate in support of the Northern Group of Armies (21st Army Group) up to and including the crossing of the Rhine.' At once, Montgomery's staff drew First Allied Airborne Army back into their plans.

Yet all plans at headquarters 21st Army Group at that moment were subsidiary still to the unsettled main issue: were they or were they not to launch the major thrust into Germany? Montgomery believed that the opportunity existed north of Aachen; and although the Canadians and the British infantry divisions were widely spread from the Seine to the Scheldt, Horrocks' XXX Corps had its armour well placed to break out. Given the fuel, this formation would soon test how far the Germans had resuscitated their defensive strength, while the remainder of the army group would be close behind. Miles Dempsey, commander of the British Second Army, shared Montgomery's confidence and proposed that he should join with Hodges and Brereton to strike across the Rhine at Wesel.

Montgomery had a more novel idea. They should lay a carpet of airborne troops across the waterways into Holland. Then, with the Rhine behind them and the Siegfried Line outflanked, the armoured formations could turn south and south-east to the Ruhr and the great open plain stretching towards Berlin. The concept had much to recommend it. The Germans would be less likely to expect an approach by this route; and the airborne army, their bases in England nicely within flying radius, would enhance surprise and bring fresh troops to the battlefield for the opening of the offensive without imposing on the local supply chain.

Anxious to obtain the support he needed in supplies for Second Army and the close co-operation of Hodges' army on his right flank, Montgomery arranged a rendezvous with the supreme commander at Brussels airfield for the afternoon of 10th September. Eisenhower did not come out from his aircraft to meet the Field-Marshal in his customary friendly way; on his return from seeing Bradley at Chartres, he had sprained his knee which was still swollen and painful. Montgomery entered with General Graham, his senior administrative staff officer. With Eisenhower was Air Chief-Marshal Tedder, his deputy, and Sir Humfrey Gale, chief administrative officer at SHAEF. Both commanders knew very well that what they had come to discuss was, in effect, the allotment of supply to the army groups.

After greetings, the Field-Marshal asked that Gale should withdraw – to which Eisenhower acceded – though surprisingly there was no suggestion to send out Graham. Then, referring to a file he had brought in which were copies of all his letters and signals to the Supreme Commander on strategic policy since the break-out began, Montgomery made a detailed analysis of the opportunities they had had, the subsequent events which confirmed these and, hence, the mistakes which the Supreme Commander had made. The Field-Marshal's manner was didactic and, as the review expanded, it began to assume the character of a master reproaching a pupil.

Eisenhower, a great heart, leaned across to put a hand on Montgomery's knee.

'Steady, Monty,' he said. 'You can't talk to me like that. I'm your boss.'

There was a silence in the aircraft. Then the Field-Marshal, great too in his own way, accepted the rebuke. 'I'm sorry, Ike,' he replied.

Talk was friendlier after that but it did not lead to either man making a major concession. Montgomery believed absolutely in the feasibility of his 'one really powerful and full-blooded thrust' into the heart of

Germany. Eisenhower feared that a single thrust by either army group would be overwhelmed, whereas the Germans would be unable to counter two delivered simultaneously over a wide arc. Patton's forces were advancing and he was not going to stop them. Montgomery too must keep up the pressure within the limits of the supplies he was receiving. In one particular, however, the Supreme Commander was prepared to give all support to Montgomery's plan: he should mount as soon as possible 'Market Garden', the airborne operation. A bridgehead across the Rhine would of course be advantageous and, as a secondary aspect, should permit allied troops to capture the V2 sites from which Hitler was launching free-flight rockets, the second of his 'secret' bombing weapons, against the south and east of England. But most important of all, Market Garden would free the estuary of the Scheldt of the German troops infesting its right bank. Their presence prevented the allies from making use of Antwerp, the third largest port in the world, one fortuitously placed to accept every form of supply they needed. Once this was opened, problems of supply would be at an end.

So the commanders parted. The Field-Marshal flew back to his headquarters assured of support to mount the airborne operation, determined in his own heart to strike into and through the Ruhr.

At the time of his appointment to command the airborne army, General Brereton had a wide range of experience in his profession. Originally a naval officer, he transferred to the United States Army and its infant flying section prior to the First World War. As an aviator, he flew against the Germans when the American Expeditionary Force came to France in 1917. After the war, a young captain, he had enjoyed a tour of duty as air attaché at the embassy in Paris. By the beginning of the Second World War, he was commanding the Third Air Force. He knew a great deal about flying and the operation of all kinds of aircraft; and he had acquired by 1944 a degree of experience in working with the British – in the Far East, in India, and through the western desert of

Lieutenant-General 'Boy' Browning, commander of the Allied 1st Airborne Corps

Egypt to French North Africa – not all of this allied relationship as pleasant as he deserved. But inevitably he knew very little about the detail of ground operations. Thus his deputy was a soldier and, in the spirit of the alliance, British. His name was F A M Browning, a Grenadier Guards officer known throughout the British Army as 'Boy'.

Lieutenant-General Browning was not called 'Boy' in a derisory way: he was much respected for his professional standards and readiness to examine and develop new ideas. Though not the founder, he was the father of British airborne forces: he brought them to maturity. Ideally, he and Brereton should have complemented each other's experience but, at quite an early stage in their relationship, there was a clash. On 3rd September, Operation Linnet II – the drop proposed in the Aachen-Maastricht gap – was brought to readiness, and Browning, as commander-designate of the airborne corps formed for the assault, met Brereton at his headquarters to receive final orders. In his diary, Brereton records:

'I told him that the operation would be mounted tomorrow or not at all. Browning brought up the point that the maps of the area could not be distributed to the lower echelons in time to brief them properly. I told him that the disorganisation of the enemy demanded that chances be taken – that the operation would not be cancelled except because of weather or direction from higher headquarters. Browning remained after the conference and told me that in his opinion the operation could not be attempted at such short notice. . . Later in the evening I received a letter from General Browning concerning our differences of opinion which concluded by saying he felt he could not continue as Deputy Commander of the First Allied Airborne Army and therefore tendered his resignation.

'(Next day) 4th September, 1944. A staff conference was held to push the completion of detailed plans for the Arnhem operation – Operation Market. Afterwards I went to Headquarters British Airborne Corps at Moor Park for a frank talk with General Browning who had cooled off considerably after writing his letter, and was quite willing to have the resignation withdrawn. He realised that under the circumstances General Ridgway (commander of the United States XVIII Airborne Corps) would command the airborne forces in Operation Linnet II. After a frank talk I felt that we understood one another.'

Operation Linnet II did not take place – Bradley at 12th Army Group having refused it – and thus no one may say certainly whether the airman or the soldier was right in this case. The weight of evidence, however, favours Browning. On what was practicable in the time, the airborne soldiers would not have been briefed by their officers until their aircraft had taken off and were en route to the

American C-47 Dakota transport aircraft on an English airfield

target area, an arrangement which at the very least would have added to the hazards of the operation. With the disagreement set aside, the two men now turned their energies to Operation Market, the most likely of the ten airborne operations under study by the planning staff.

The early conferences for Market, from 4th September onwards, were primarily concerned with what could be offered operationally. The first limitation was the number of transport aircraft available in Major-General Paul L Williams' United States IX Troop Carrier Command, and the Royal Air Force 38 and 46 Groups under Air Vice-Marshal 'Holly' Hollinghurst and Air Commodore L Darvell. Between them, supposing all their hopes for servicing to be well-founded, they would offer 1,250 C-47 Dakotas and a mixed bag of 354 converted British bombers. It did not take an advanced mathematician to show that this quantity would not lift all the parachutists, tow all the assorted gliders of more than two divisions. But the distance from the forward lines of the British Second Army on the Meuse-Escaut canal to Arnhem in Holland was ninety-eight miles and there were six major waterways to be crossed before they were over the Rhine. The very least that Browning needed for his airborne carpet was three and a half divisions.

Major-General James M Gavin

Major-General Maxwell D Taylor

There were five divisions to choose from: the American 82nd (All American), the 101st (Screaming Eagles) and the newly arrived 17th; the British 1st and 6th Airborne. In addition, Major-General Stanislas Sosabowski's Independent Polish Parachute Brigade was anxious to join in the battles of north-west Europe. So indeed were they all. But the British 1st Airborne had seen no action since Sicily. Hence they were selected. As the 17th had not had time to work up, General Ridgway, commander of the XVIII Airborne Corps, offered the 82nd and 101st. The commanders of these three divisions, with Sosabowski, were now secretly warned of the commitment.

IX Troop Carrier Command under Major-General Paul L Williams had a cadre of four groups which had acquired a variety of experience in the Mediterranean, dropping British and American parachutists in North Africa and both parachutists and gliders in Sicily. Prior to D-day, they had returned to England to join with a further ten groups sent as reinforcements directly from the United States. There was an intensive training period before the Normandy assault but it was inadequate for the difficult task of finding in darkness the dropping zones for the parachutists, the landing zones for the gliders, with the added distraction of enemy anti-aircraft fire. Only twenty-five per cent of the 82nd and 101st were dropped in the correct areas – hence General Eisenhower's directions that navigation skills must be developed.

The command was very conscious that their mission was, primarily, combat despite the fact that they operated air transport. After D-day, they returned to training keenly. Yet, as operations failed to materialise, they could not forget that beyond all else their purpose was flying. Due to the restriction of exercises, air crew hours were far lower in the Troop Carrier Command than those in fighter or bombardment squadrons and certainly less than those in the transport squadrons committed permanently to logistics. Air and ground crews were not therefore as downcast as their commander when, squadron by squadron, they were drawn to France.

General Brereton had no doubts, however, that if the airborne army was to be ready to mount operations at short notice, his airmen must practise, practise, practise for combat. It took much hard work on his part, sometimes hard words, to recover, hold and set to training the continually shifting squadrons. They had scarcely completed the first phase of his preparatory programme when Market was decided upon.

Air-Commodore Darvell's six squadrons of Dakotas – 46 Group – and Air

Major-General Roy Urquhart

Major-General Stanislas Sosabowski

Vice-Marshal Hollinghurst's 38 Group of converted bombers were better placed. The latter had been engaged in the development of British airborne forces since 1941 and had acquired a depth of knowledge in the techniques of aerial delivery. Darvell's aircraft, though latecomers to this work, were not subject to diversion to the extent suffered by IX Troop Carrier Command. Both of the Royal Air Force groups had launched troops successfully by night and their subsequent training had enhanced their confidence. At Browning's instigation, a standard procedure had been adopted for all allied airborne troops so that the Royal Air Force could readily – and did – exercise with American troops, the United States Army Air Corps with British.

The 82nd and 101st Divisions had much in common, the latter having been formed from a cadre of the first. The commander of the 82nd was Brigadier-General Jim Gavin, a former enlisted man, a graduate of West Point and a rising star in the allied forces. Aged 37, he had been a captain in 1941, a volunteer member of the Provisional Parachute Group at Fort Benning, Georgia. When the 82nd jumped into Sicily in 1943, he was with them, commanding a regiment. In Normandy, he was deputy to Matt Ridgway, then commanding the 82nd; and understandably he had succeeded him when Ridgway was promoted to command XVIII Airborne Corps. Maxwell D Taylor, his colleague in the 101, was a gunner, former artillery chief of the 82nd in Sicily and in command of the 101st in Normandy.

Each of their divisions retained a strong cadre of men who had jumped in either or both the Mediterranean and Normandy but these operations and training accidents in their turn had removed a significant number from their units, particularly experienced leaders. Thus, while they were mature in comparison with the 17th Airborne Division, every man was aware of the need to train hard in readiness for the battlefield. In the south-west of England the 101st, and in the north midlands the 82nd were never idle during that summer of 1944, whether engaged in rigorous advanced exercises or in the necessary routine of drill, weapon handling, and other basic skills. Because the majority were volunteers, their response to this taxing work was prompt and willing. They were aware of being a *corps d'élite*; men who had stepped out of the mass to be committed not only quickly to the battlefield but to some crucial task on it. It was a paradox that they, like their British airborne comrades, should discover that they were destined more often to remain in the rear as a special reserve.

The British 1st Airborne Division

33

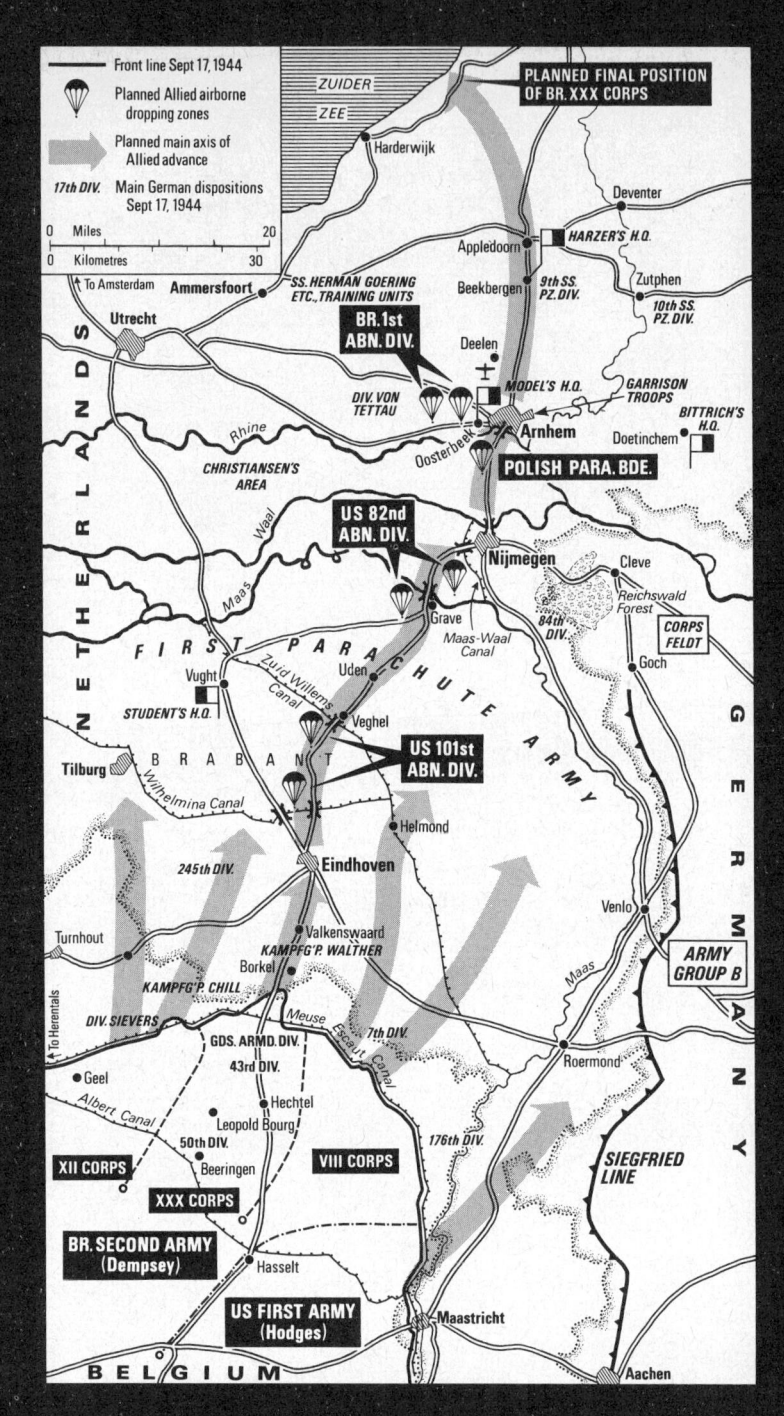

Dispositions of the opposing forces at the beginning of Operation 'Market Garden'.

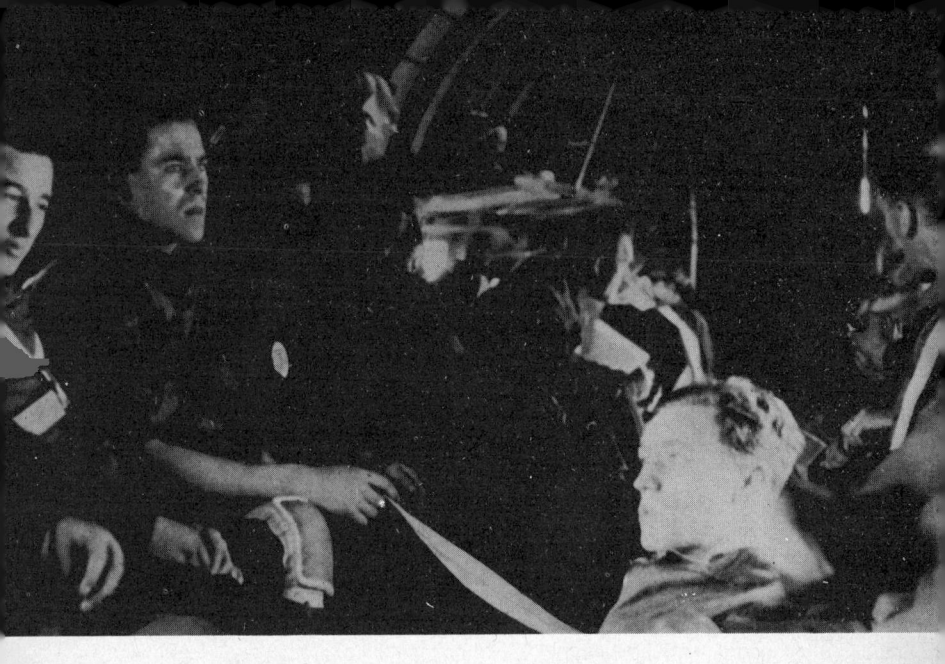

British airborne troops en route for Tunisia in November 1942. Those who returned formed the veteran nucleus of the 1st Airborne Division

had, like the 82nd and 101st, a strong cadre of veterans. A British parachute battalion had been raised in 1941 under Lieutenant-Colonel Eric Down and two others had formed quickly thereafter. Raids had been conducted by these parachutists into Italy and France early in 1942 and when the allies landed in French North Africa the parachute brigade, carried in American C-47s, leap-frogged through Algeria into Tunisia. It was a unique body, having as many university graduates amongst the enlisted men as former labourers. They fought on a divisional front when the Germans struck back, earning the nickname *roten teufeln*, red devils, when, wearing their red berets, they knocked Arnim's Panzer Grenadiers off a series of hill tops. Joined by the remainder of the division, they jumped into Sicily and landed by sea in Italy. Then, shedding a brigade, the division came home for Christmas, 1943, had a happy leave, took in recruits and stood by for a battle call.

Month after month, there was none. 6th Airborne Division departed for Normandy. Again and again, the 1st were briefed to follow them to France but on every occasion the advancing troops overran the target area before their aircraft took off. There was a growing recklessness in the division; a danger of ill-discipline in wild parties following cancellation of operations. Their disappointment and a serious loss of morale was prevented only by the close spirit of the officers and men in the division, particularly those who had served together since early days.

When Eric Down, the first battalion commander, since promoted to command the division, left to raise airborne forces in India, his successor was, surprisingly, a major-general who had no knowledge of their speciality. His name was Roy Urquhart, an officer of the Highland Light Infantry, modest, straightforward, who had earned his spurs as a deliberate tactician in Sicily and Italy. He confessed to air-sickness, omitted to get himself trained as a parachutist, yet won the respect of his command because he was sound and sincere.

Unfortunately, he did not recognise that, while there is no mystique in airborne forces, certain characteristics are inherent in them as in all arms of a military body. Unfortunately for himself – and for them.

The plan is made

On Saturday, 9th September, 'Boy' Browning was in Belgium at Field-Marshal Montgomery's advanced headquarters. He was to be briefed on the 21st Army Group plan; more precisely, the Field-Marshal's concept of the operation.

Montgomery had not then received Eisenhower's assent – it was on the following day that they met at Brussels airfield – but he wanted to advance preparations as he was supremely aware that every day of respite given to the enemy must reduce the allies' chance of victory in 1944.

He began by reiterating the aim of Market: 'to capture and hold the crossings over the canals and rivers on the Second Army's main axis of advance from about Eindhoven to Arnhem inclusive.' As soon as the airborne carpet was down, Operation Garden was to begin. The British XXX Corps would push forward from the Meuse-Escaut canal with a strong force of armour; on its left a British corps would follow up to protect the eastern flank. To the west, it was expected that General Hodges would launch covering operations in parallel with XXX Corps.

At the end of the briefing, the Field Marshal returned to the subject of th bridges. Dotting the bridge symbol on the map in succession, he remarked 'The (airborne) carpet is very long s it will necessarily be narrow. Th essence of the business is to captur those bridges intact. And this wil mean,' the finger dotted the bridge again, 'dropping as many men on t the bridges as possible from the wor "go".'

'How long do you think we shal have to hold the bridge at Arnhem? asked Browning.

'Two days,' said the Field-Marshal 'They should be up to you by then.'

'We can hold it for four,' said Browning, 'But I think we may be going bridge too far.'

Next day, Sunday the 10th, Browning gave outline orders to the divi sional commanders at his head quarters in the club house of Moo Park golf course, a little to the nort and west of London.

The southern area of the 'carpet' wa given to the 101st because they wer

The US 82nd Airborne Division practising a mass drop

36

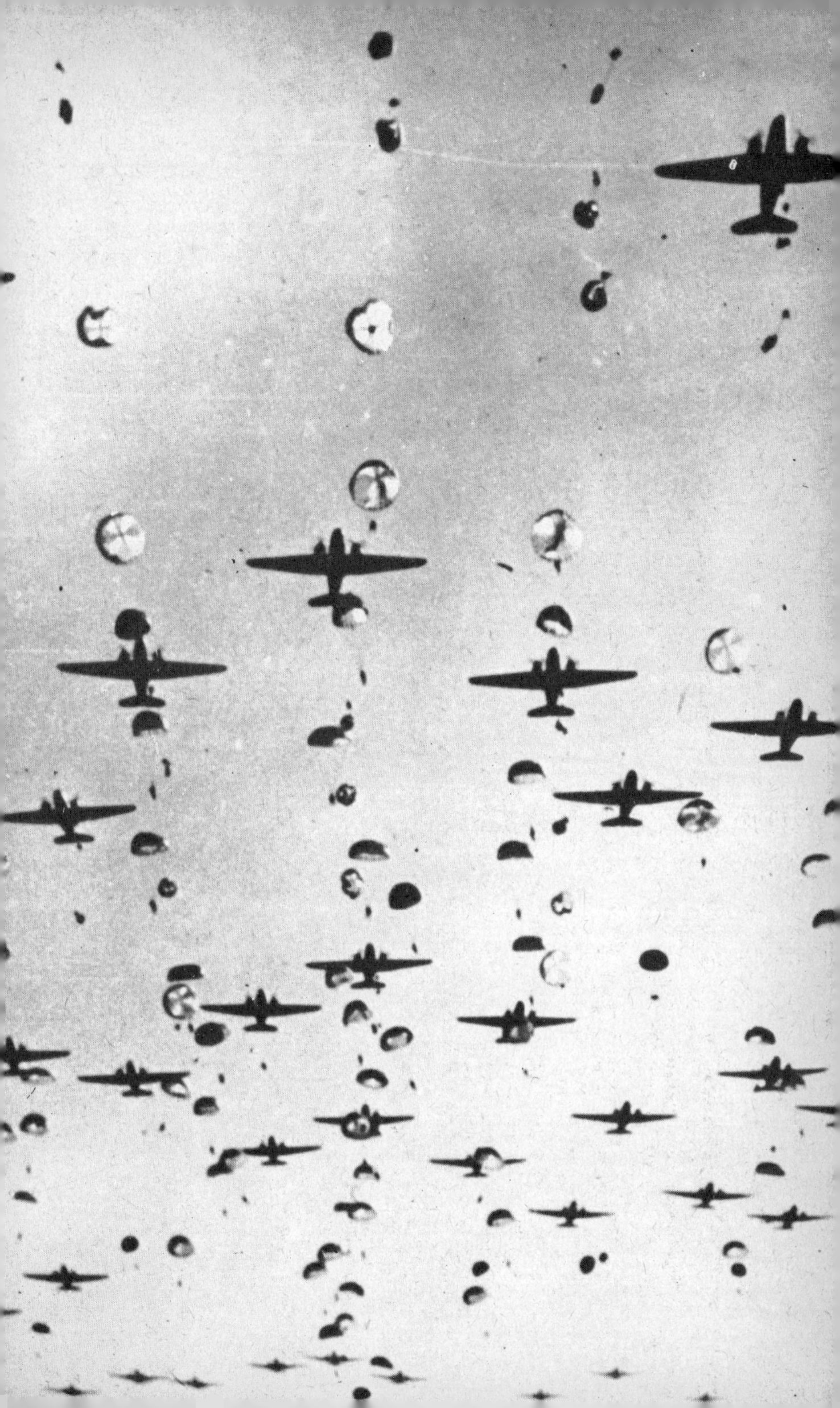

stationed in south-west England. In consequence, they would be able to fly to their release point without crossing the aircraft stream of other divisions. General Taylor was not happy when he heard the suggestion – originating with the Field-Marshal – that he should drop in seven packets alongside the major and minor bridges but, immediately, he said nothing.

Next, the 82nd were directed to seize the bridges over the Maas at Grave and the Waal at Nijmegen. Between these bridges, the road was dominated by high ground, rare in Holland, and this too was to be captured and prepared for defence.

In the extreme north, 1st Airborne were to land at Arnhem. General Browning drew a large circle round the river crossing and city on his briefing map.

'Arnhem Bridge,' he said, turning to Urquhart, 'And hold it.'

In the days after the war, there has been some argument as to why the British were selected for the distant objective. American historians have noted that the British specially requested the most difficult mission; other opinions correctly say that Urquhart and his staff had been examining the area under a previous plan – Operation Comet – and infer that it was logical that they should use this knowledge for Market. There appears to be no record as to why the decision was taken. A simple explanation is that, since the 101st were, for ease of flying routes, placed in the south, it was expedient to place the 82nd next to them. In any case, no one could forecast where the principal danger would lie.

So Urquhart's division was ordered to take and hold Arnhem bridge, and a bridgehead on the far side to facilitate the expansion beyond the Rhine of the divisions in Horrocks' XXX Corps. Because of the distance, General Browning placed the Polish brigade as a reinforcement to Urquhart's command. To strengthen further the bridgehead across the Rhine, the 52nd Lowland Scottish Division was briefed to be ready to land next to 1st Airborne as soon as an American engineer battalion prepared aircraft landing strips. If all went well, six divisions would be across the Rhine within three days of the airborne assault.

On 11th September, however, all was not going well in Field-Marshal Montgomery's view. As ordered by 12th Army Group, General Hodges was both trying to maintain a continuous front between Dempsey's Second Army on his left and Patton's Third on his right – a front of 150 miles – and to advance through the Siegfried Line wherever resistance was minimal. Inevitably, his divisions were out of balance. Through no fault of his own, he could not co-ordinate a close action with Dempsey or offer a force to protect the eastern flank of Horrocks' advance. Thus, at a late hour, Dempsey had to bring another of his own corps, the VIII, for this latter task. But VIII Corps were on the Seine, immobile, stripped of their trucks, which were being used to carry forward supplies for Operation Garden.

'I have investigated my maintenance situation very carefully since our meeting yesterday,' the Field-Marshal signalled to the Supreme Commander personally. 'Your decision that the northern thrust toward the Ruhr is NOT repeat NOT to have priority over other operations will have certain repercussions. . .' He spelt out Dempsey's dilemma, adding: 'The large scale operations by Second Army and the Airborne Corps northwards towards the Meuse and Rhine cannot now take place before 23rd September at the earliest and possibly 26th September.'

It was evident to Eisenhower and his Chief-of-Staff, General Bedell Smith, that this was no exaggeration. On the 12th, Bedell Smith came forward to Montgomery's headquarters; for if there was agreement on nothing else, none doubted that if they were to secure a Rhine crossing cheaply, it must be done quickly. There was besides the need to isolate and crush German resistance in the area of Antwerp. Patton would be told to stand on the defensive, said Bedell Smith; the bulk of 12th Army Group's logistic support would be given to Hodges's First Army, with whom 21st Army Group might deal directly. United States truck companies would be switched from the Red Ball express routes to carry forward supplies at the rate of an additional 500 tons per day and transport aircraft would bring up another 500. As quickly as possible, a bomber force would be gathered to lift motor spirit to Liège.

With these assurances, Montgomery signalled to Eisenhower on 14th September, 'Most grateful to you personally and Beetle (Bedell Smith) for all you are doing for us.' He confirmed that, subject to weather, Market Garden should begin on 17th September, as he had originally intended.

In England, all the essential planning decisions had been taken.

The allocation of aircraft had rightly favoured the two American divisions. If they were delivered in inadequate numbers, they could not capture the bridges or the high ground near Nijmegen and XXX Corps would have no chance of reaching Arnhem speedily. This left Urquhart with a lift for one of his three parachute brigades, part of the glider brigade and his advanced divisional headquarters – one third his total force. To offset this disadvantage, Air Vice-Marshal Hollinghurst suggested that they should release the troops in the darkness of the early morning before the

The British Horsa Glider

dawn mists rose. This would permit a second lift by the air transport force in daylight on the 17th besides possessing the advantage of enhancing secrecy and deception.

General Brereton did not like this proposal. The American air crews, as he knew to his vexation, had not had time to train to the standards of night navigation he had set. With such a narrow corridor, with time so much at a premium, accuracy in delivery was essential to success. At night, too, the slow Dakotas would be vulnerable to German night fighters, still active, and the flak batteries could not be struck effectively immediately prior to the passage of the long streams of aircraft. The fuel tanks of the Dakotas were not self-sealing; the risk of substantial losses before reaching the target area was consequently high.

He therefore ruled that the aircraft should take off as soon as practicable after first light on the 17th.

When it was suggested that they might still make a second drop on the

17th, he continued to resist but with scarcely the same weight of reason. Even if they could not get back in daylight – which some believed possible – the flak batteries would have been struck throughout the day and the troops on the ground would be able to guide aircraft to them by beacons. Yet General Brereton persisted that only one lift should be attempted on the 17th, now citing crew fatigue, the need for spot servicing and emergency repair to support his decision. He attempted to comfort the soldiers with the assurances of his planning staff that the entire force would be delivered by D plus 2; but whatever comfort they derived from it grew cold when detailed calculations showed that the earliest date for completion must be D plus 3. Nevertheless, Brereton persisted in his decision. What he overlooked was the fact that the operation was being mounted with one aim alone: securing the ground corridor across the Rhine. The air transport operation was not an end in itself but a means to an end: an airborne assault. This method offered complete surprise and hence shock action. But the effect of the shock would diminish with every hour that passed after the initial daylight drop took place. The view that the air plan would ensure each following morning air crew and aircraft fresh and fit for operations was a blind one. If Taylor did not receive speedily his artillery and glider infantry or Gavin the balance of parachute and glider infantry and certain follow up field and anti-tank batteries; and above all, if Urquhart did not receive directly the two thirds of his force left behind, the probability was that the initiative gained by surprise would be lost to the enemy.

Even if this most cogent argument did not persuade Brereton to agree to a double delivery on D-day, it is surely curious that, as an airman, he failed to see that however slick he expected air operations to be, he could not control the weather, which in the third week of September might prevent follow up deliveries over several days.

British paratroops practise dropping from the converted RAF Whitley bomber

As General Brereton's decision to restrict the sortie rate reduced the chances of success, General Urquhart's arrangements tended to confound them. Rightly, he had begun by asking to have his force put down as close to his objectives as possible. The RAF objected to a dropping zone close to the Arnhem bridge and to other areas to the east of the town due to flak positions on the run-in or on the exit routes or both. A Dutch officer – there were Dutch liaison teams with each division – advised that the polder or fenland below the west bank of the Rhine was likely to be soft and was in any case intersected by numerous wide drainage ditches. Opposed by the strong objections of the air force and the opinion of a native of Holland, Urquhart gave way. Regretfully, he chose dropping and landing zones six and eight miles to the west and a little to the north of Arnhem. As a compromise, he obtained agreement to dropping the Poles on the polder one mile south of the bridge on the third day of the assault; it being expected that the flak in the immediate vicinity would have been cleared by the time of their arrival and perhaps in some of the other areas. The objections concerning the suitability of the polder had therefore been overcome. Its marshy surface and ditches were no longer considered unsurmountable. The flak batteries on the run-in and the formidable concentration on Deelen airfield to the north of Arnhem appear also to have become acceptable; for there could be no certainty that, by D plus 2, these would have been destroyed from the air or overrun on the ground.

The cause of Urquhart's difficulties is not difficult to discern. In the planning of any airborne assault, it is the duty of the air force commander to state forcefully what circumstances he needs to deliver and release the troops so that they begin the ground operation from the areas selected with the maximum strength in men and equipment. Inevitably, as in the planning for Arnhem, some of the requirements of the air force would clash with those of the army. There should then follow a phase of discussion in order to effect the best compromise – each of the parties knowing or coming to realise as the discussion proceeds that matters of principle cannot in any circumstances be surrendered. If Urquhart had been an experienced airborne divisional commander, he would have known that the location of dropping and landing zones to targets is a prime factor of success. If the RAF had persisted in refusal to drop anywhere close to the bridge and city, it would have been his duty to state that the operation must be abandoned from the soldier's point of view, having too low a chance of success. But Urquhart was not experienced and did not put to his air colleagues such a charge. It is very unlikely indeed that either Hollinghurst, commanding the air element for the Arnhem drop, or his American colleagues, would have refused simply because of the danger of flying into flak – there is no record of either the RAF or the United States Army Air Force ever refusing an operational hazard of this sort in the Second World War or since, when it was shown to be necessary. Yet it is scarcely fair to burden General Urquhart with all the blame. He did not volunteer for his command but was surprised by it. It was a misguided appointment, particularly so when there were to hand Brigadiers Lathbury and Hackett commanding the 1st and 4th Parachute Brigades in the division, each of whom was recommended for divisional command. Indeed, Gerald Lathbury, the senior, had been informed that he was to be promoted to go to the Indian division, while Down stayed with the 1st.

The fact was, however, that by 13th September, 1st Airborne Division was committed to landing six or eight miles to the west of Arnhem between the roads leading to Amsterdam and Utrecht. To get to the bridge, they would have to pass through a town – Oosterbeek – or make a detour, either course adding to the time needed to satisfy the principal requirement: the capture of the Rhine crossing.

None of those attending the divisional commander's conference on the afternoon of Tuesday, 12th September, raised any demur at the orders given. This is not surprising; for Urquhart and his staff disclosed the reasons for the shortfall in aircraft and the

41

Parachute soldier in a gusting wind after landing

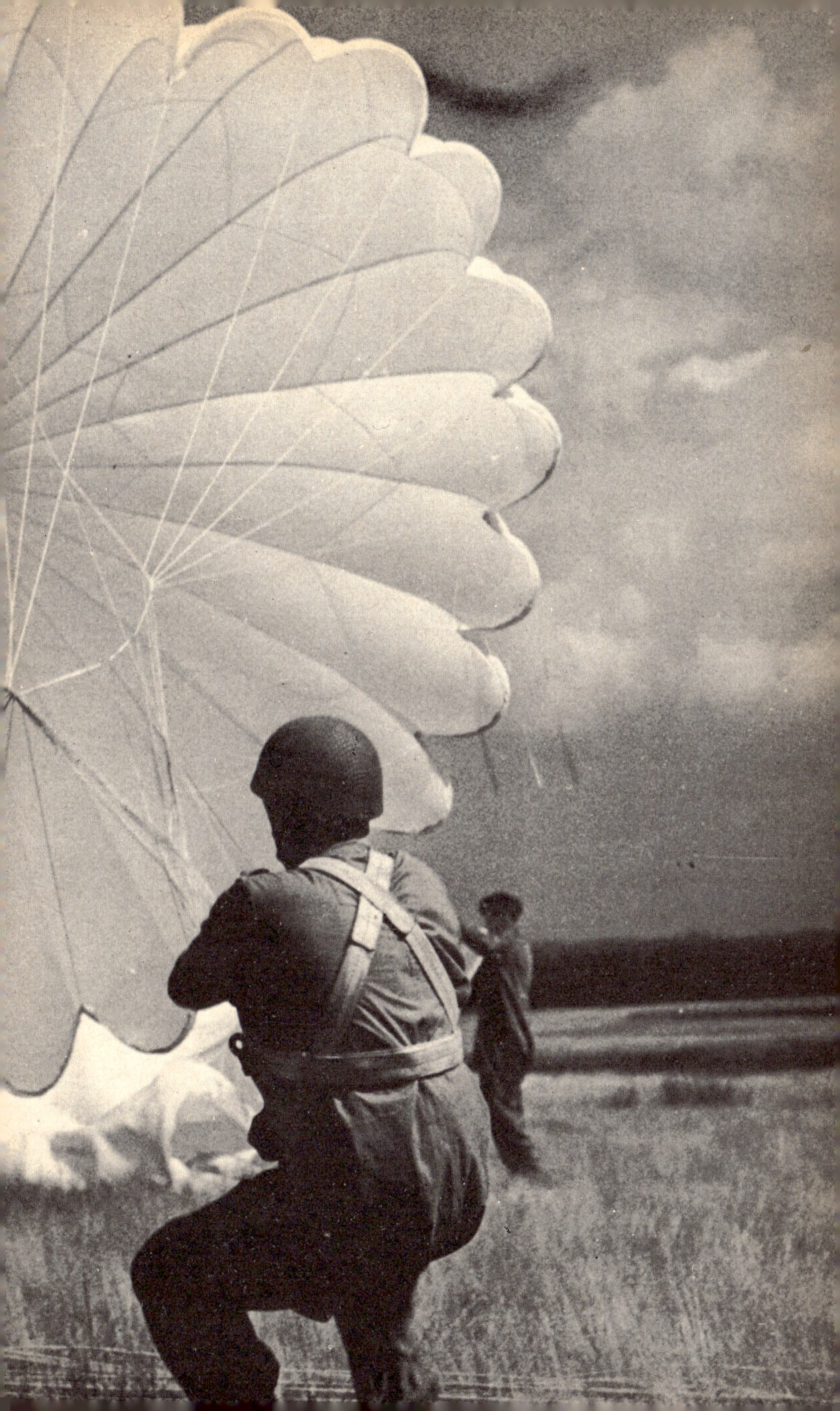

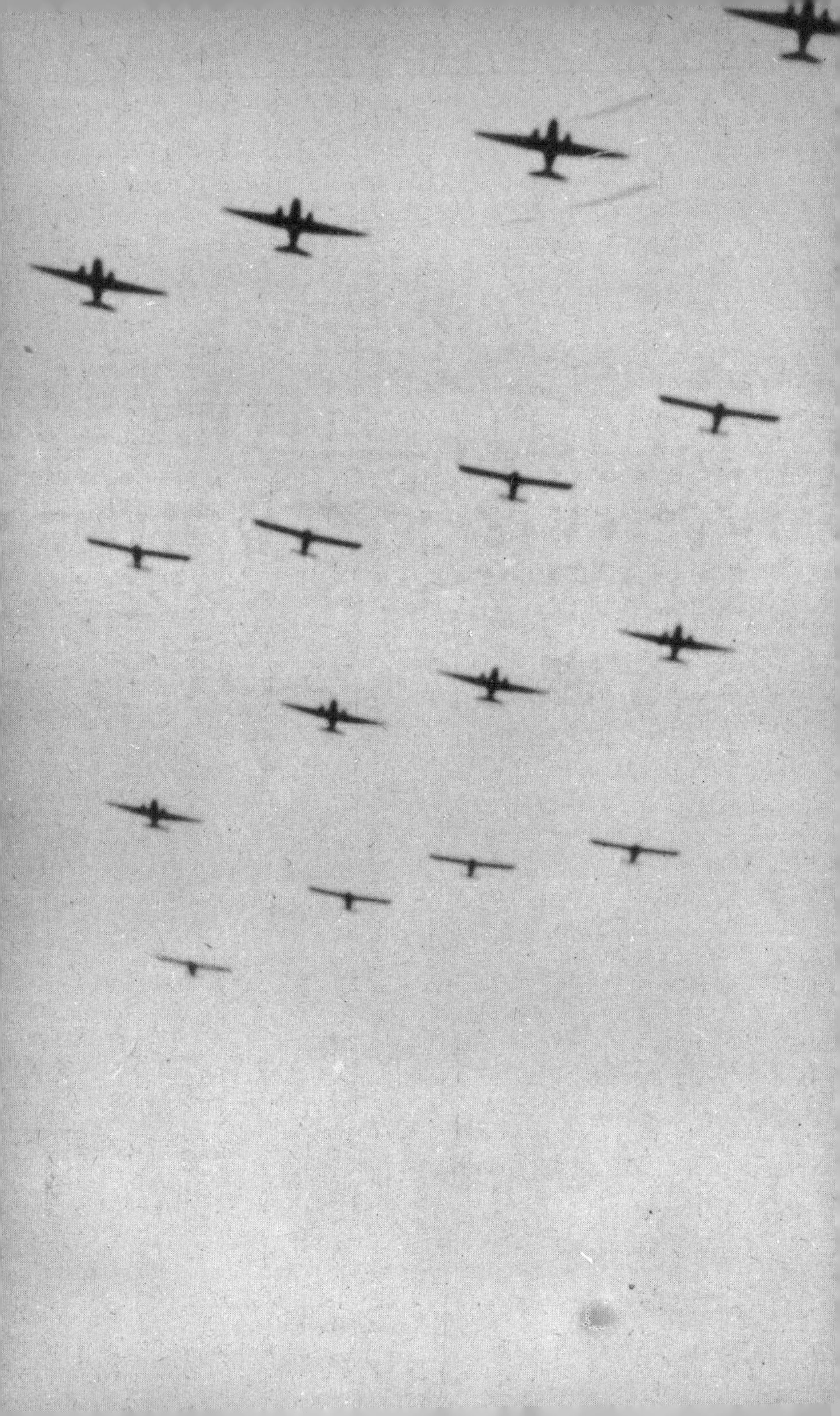

objections' of the RAF to dropping elsewhere. Moreover, if the truth be told, none of those present had any certainty that the operation would take place. They had all planned numerous operations previously – some far more risky than Market – and they would have been less than human had they been immune to the effects of cancellation after cancellation. It was not that they did not take their preparations seriously; simply that their recent experience suggested that they might well be indulging in another theoretical exercise.

The commanders of the 82nd and 101st were less inhibited. Though they had also planned numerous operations without execution, they had operated as recently as June and the memories of what had gone well, what had gone badly were more sharply etched on their professional minds. Jim Gavin and Browning had close discussions concerning the high ground immediately south-east of Nijmegen. Progressively, its importance was borne upon both of them; the capture of the bridges at Grave and Nijmegen would be nullified if the enemy possessed it. Adjoining it to the east, towards Cleve and Goch, the Reichswald Forest was seen to be an area in which the enemy might well be concealed and from which an early German counter-attack would be dangerous. It was even possible that German troops might be conducting refresher training on the high ground; they were known to use if for this purpose, as the Dutch had done in the days before the war.

Maxwell D Taylor had other apprehensions. After the initial co-ordinating conference at Headquarters, First Allied Airbone Army, he raised with Browning objections concerning the dropping of his force in seven packets on to each of the bridges in his area. Though fully in agreement that the division must drop close to its targets, he believed they were going too much to the other extreme. There was a danger that the groups on first landing would be too weak at one point or another to overcome an enemy in prepared defences such as the steel and concrete posts picked up from the photographs provided by air reconnaissance; perhaps even too weak to resist a local counterattack. But General Browning would not change the requirement since he had agreed to it personally with Field-Marshal Montgomery and the matter was referred to Brereton, whose relationship with his British corps commander again came under strain.

'I decided', General Brereton wrote in his diary on 11th September, 'that General Taylor would see Montgomery about a more concentrated landing. If, after the disadvantages of the first manoeuver have been explained (to him), he still insists, we will go in as planned.'

Contrary to their expectation, yet characteristically, Montgomery had no wish to interfere with or impose personal ideas on the detail of the ground plan. If they had any doubts, however, they should be discussed with Dempsey. The diary goes on:

'13th September 1944. General Parks (Brereton's Chief-of-Staff) who went with Taylor to the 21st Army Group, reported that Lieutenant-General Sir Miles C Dempsey, commanding the British Second Army, was in accord with our recommendations for changes in Operation Market. General Dempsey seems to have a better appreciation of the employment of airborne forces than any other British ground commander. He is not only a competent soldier but he has a delightful personality – quiet, unassuming and exceedingly modest.'

Careful arrangements were made to preserve secrecy.

Until 15th September, knowledge of the operations was restricted in the airborne corps to those normally present at a divisional commander's orders with the addition of a few staff officers at the lower headquarters. By this stage in their wartime lives, each formation, each unit had a special set of rooms secured by locks and wire in which plans were made. Only those named on a special list held at the entrance were permitted to pass inside. On the 15th, battalion commanders and officers were admitted to the secret; on the 16th, the soldiers were briefed. Camps and barracks were then sealed, though special

C 47 Transports and gliders training in close formation flying

45

Above: Lieutenant-General Sir Brian Horrocks, commander of XXX Corps, who led the British Armoured column along the carpet to the Rhine. *Far right:* A wrecked V-1 launching site

arrangements were made to send a number of selected men out to local towns and villages under caution so that the word should not spread through the British countryside that Americans, Poles and British airborne soldiers were concentrating for an operation.

In Belgium, General Horrocks, commander of XXX Corps in Dempsey's army, did not brief his subordinates for Operation Garden until the 15th. At 11 o'clock that morning, in the small garrison town of Bourg Leopold, he entered the cinema which was surrounded by military police and field security detachments.

Because he had left his own briefing until a late hour in the interest of secrecy; because the operation was of a special and complex nature; and because he was a man who liked above all to maintain a personal contact with those he commanded, Horrocks had all the officers of his corps down to the rank of lieutenant-colonel present for the briefing, and the brigade majors – principal staff officers – of the armoured and infantry brigades.

A tall man, with shining silver hair worn rather long, he walked to the front of the auditorium, lightly greeting many officers by name. On the stage, which he ascended, a large sketch map had been placed. It was now uncovered.

There was complete silence as eyes read, consumed the information disclosed: the thin corridor running northwards through Borken and Valkenswaard to Eindhoven; the symbols showing the dropping zones of the 101st and their objectives beyond; the road running on to Grave and Nijmegen; the Maas, the Maas/Waal canal, the Waal, the high ground to the east of the road, all in the area of the 82nd; and beyond, the Rhine, Arnhem and 1st Airborne with the Poles.

'This is a tale you will tell your grandchildren,' Horrocks began. Then fearing this sounded too dramatic, he added, 'and mighty bored they'll be.'

Horrocks was a sensitive and imaginative officer. He had developed successfully his own method of commanding a corps in fast, mobile warfare in the North African desert; and had then devised a single sledgehammer tactic for crushing the strong defences round Tunis and Bizerta before he was gravely wounded. He had now to explain a form of breakout novel to them all. Simply, they had to do a hop, skip and a jump over obstacles of unknown type, aided by the stepping stones secured by their airborne comrades.

As soon as the airborne assault began, Horrocks would personally give the signal to start. The Guards Armoured Division must then rush forward, destroying or sweeping away the enemy between its bridgehead across the Meuse-Escaut canal and Eindhoven. Then on again, through Nijmegen and Arnhem. The narrowness of the front was emphasised – it could scarcely accommodate more than one tank battalion with infantry support at any one time, so they must be slick in passing units through one another as the leaders took casualties and lost the pace. Horrocks' tactical headquarters would be close behind and then the 43rd Wessex and the 50th Northumbrian Infantry Divisions. With only one major road, close control of traffic would be essential. Traffic posts linked by radio would extend north from the hour of starting; each stretch of the road would be allotted recovery trucks to pull clear tanks or trucks broken down or hit by enemy fire. The engineers were putting all their bridging material on trucks ready to come forward to any bridge or culvert blown. Supply traffic, other than for ammunition, was forbidden: they should cram on enough food for four days, motor fuel for 250 miles, and jettison anything that was not essential for the short operation.

'It has to be short,' said Horrocks. 'If it isn't, we shall fail those parachutists. They are relying on us.'

His officers left the cinema much stimulated by their briefing. All felt that they were in the mind of their corps commander. Knowing his aim, it would be easier to make their own contribution to Garden. As ever, without minimising the difficulties, Horrocks radiated optimism and they reflected this spirit. All the same,

'The Germans seem to be thickening up a bit,' remarked one commanding officer to a colleague.

'Perhaps it's just as well we're not leaving them any longer to reorganise,' was the reply.

47

Briefing

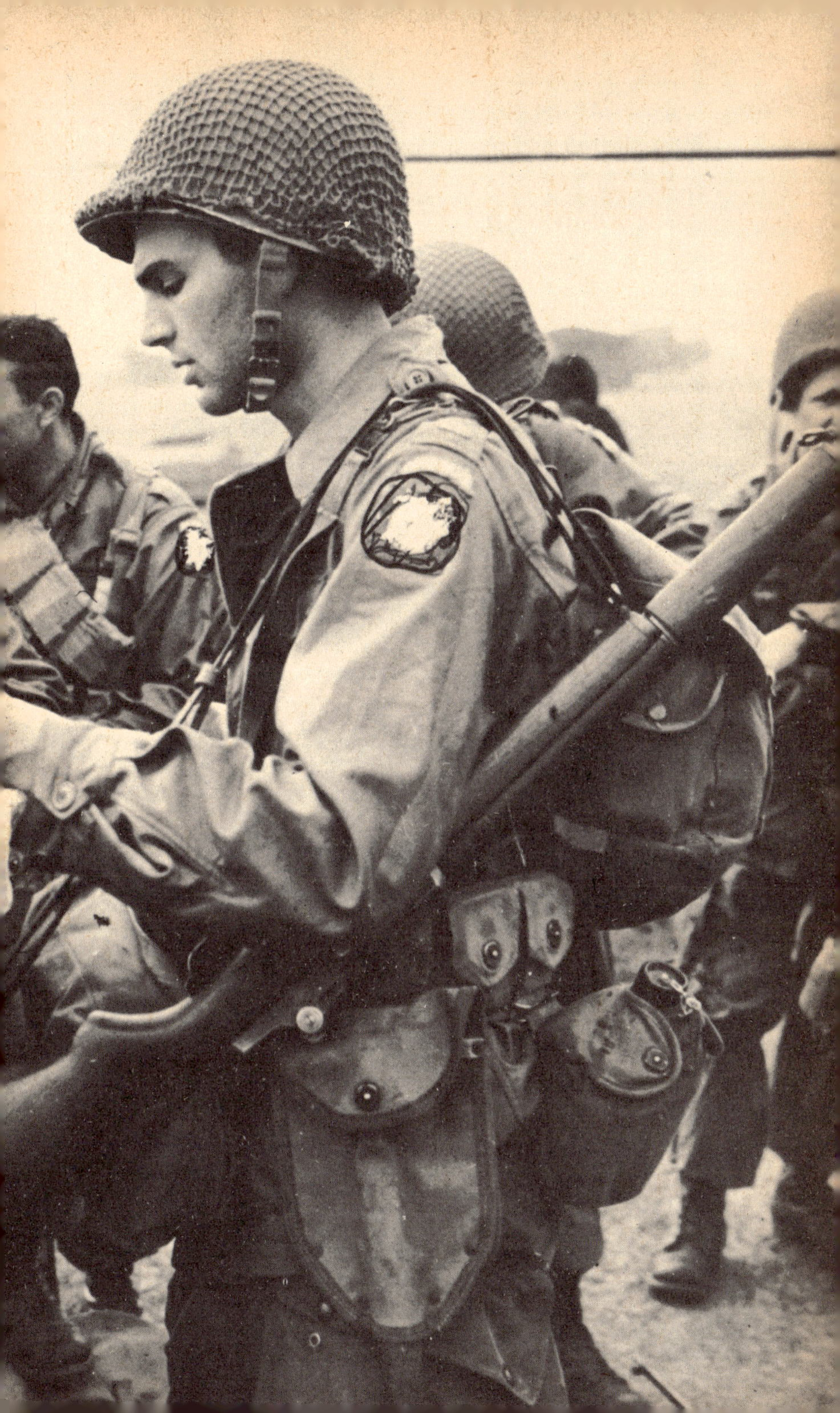

Airspeed Horsa Mk II
Span: 88 feet *Length:* 67 feet *Crew:* Two *Load:* 29 troops or one 75mm pack howitzer

Douglas C-47 Dakota
Speed: 230 mph maximum and 167 mph cruising *Range:* 1,300 miles *Crew:* Three *Load:* 9,028 lbs of cargo, 18/24 paratroopers or one glider

51

'Whence this strange intelligence?'

On the night of 3rd September, Field-Marshal Model's operational report represented again his critical need of reinforcement. Horrocks' corps was about to enter Antwerp. Between the city port and the Ardennes, on an arc of 150 miles to the south-east, a few weak German detachments occupied portions of the West Wall defences or watched the major bridges across the Albert Canal and the Maas river. They could not be sure whether the enemy had already come up to and passed between their positions; for there were gaps of ten and more miles between posts. In the north, the remnant of Fifteenth Army had been driven back to the Scheldt estuary. Sixty miles to the south, a cloud of defeated, disorganised groups, formerly the Seventh Army, was moving across the countryside, veering now north-eastward towards the borders of Holland and Germany to avoid being run down by Hodges' army.

The immediate requirement to man and hold a defence line to the Ardennes, Model reported, was '... twenty-five fresh divisions with an adequate armoured reserve of five to six Panzer divisions ... otherwise the gateway into north-west Germany will be open.'

When this signal was received at Hitler's headquarters in East Prussia on the morning of 4th September, the staff could offer the Führer no suggestions as to where even one fresh division might be found. Nothing could be spared from Russia. Italy had been cut beyond the minimum requirement of its commander for defence. Certain Panzer divisions, spent to exhaustion in the east, were reforming as brigades but were unable to be moved. Himmler's new *volksgrenadier* divisions were still enrolling schoolboys and pensioners. As a desperate expedient, it was decided to send Model 'battalions' as individual units, comprised of training staffs, police, storemen, pioneer labour, Todt workers of all nationalities, hospital convalescents. The navy was stripped of men in shore establishments. Coastal batteries were ordered to send half their manpower. Even the flak regiments

General Student inspecting parachute troops

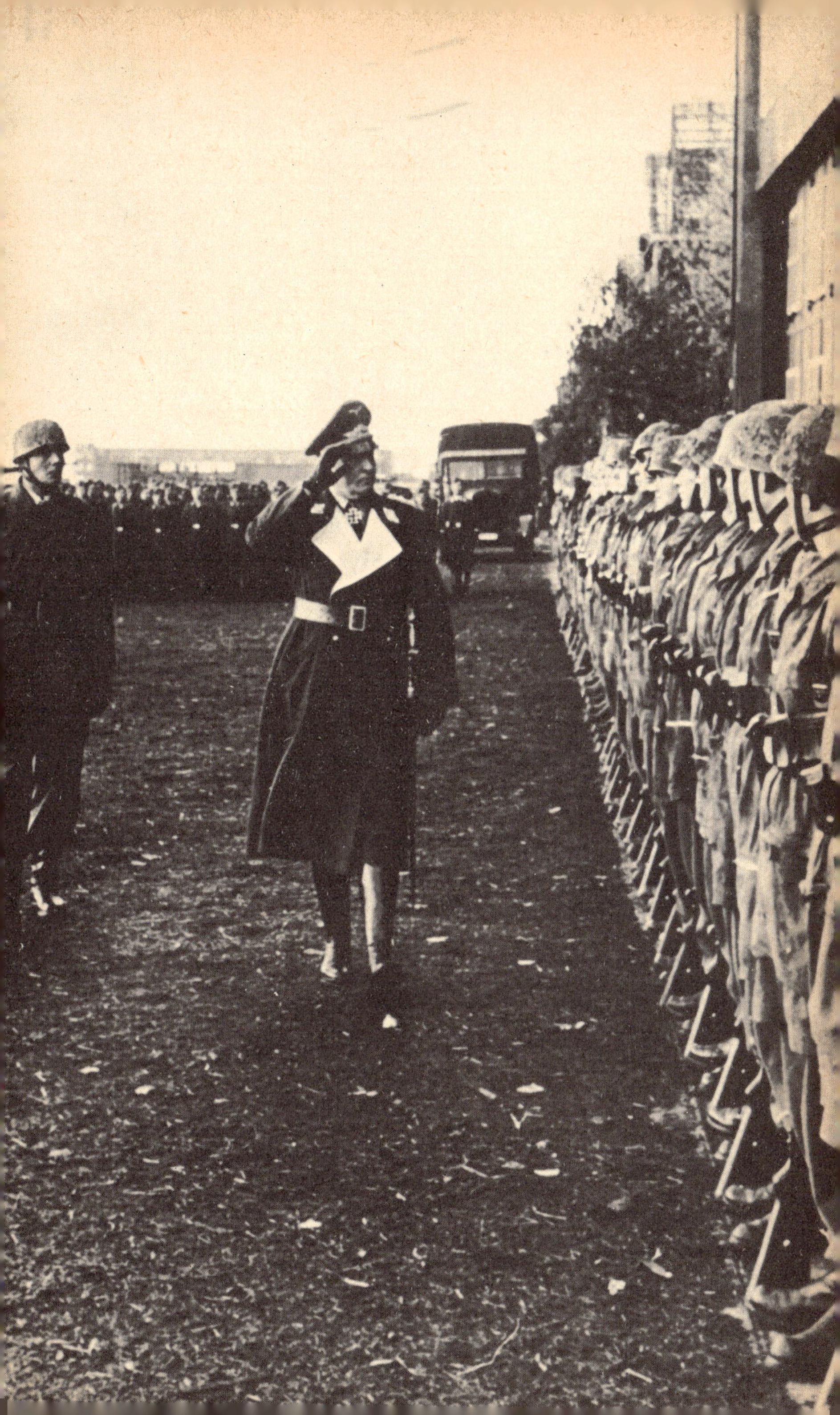

The crossing of the Albert Canal. Tanks and transport cross the bridge put up by engineers

were obliged to find a quota for the western front. The sum of these measures was 135,000, 150 'battalions', the infantry for twenty-five divisions. Though the figure was impressive, the army staff knew very well that, even when they were organised and moved, the presence of these units would be of value only to thicken a defence line already formed and controlled.

There was thus some relief when Göring announced on the 4th that he had to offer an 'army' already forming, much of it in being. He referred to the six parachute regiments training and reorganising after operations, some of whose battalions had been almost completely reconstituted by trainees. The convalescent depots should yield a further two regiments, making a total of 20,000 troops. To these he would add a further 10,000 officers and men from air and ground crews, station staffs and signals who were idle because of the shortage of fuel for the Luftwaffe squadrons. Under General Karl Student, Commander-in-Chief of German airborne forces, they would constitute the First Parachute Army. That afternoon, Göring telephoned Student, who was in Berlin, and told him to report as soon as possible to the commander of Army Group B.

Meantime, Model was watching anxiously the forces he had deployed in an effort to stem the allied advance.

At the beginning of September, there was only one division in Holland, the 719th, comprised of fit men over forty-five and others, younger, unfit for full service in the field. Its task was coast defence. In August, its mobility had been improved by a reinforcement of horses impressed from the Dutch populace; its ranks filled out by Luftwaffe ground staffs. This was the force sent into Belgium to halt Horrocks.

The senior and elderly general commanding the division, Karl Sievers, decided to dig his defences on the north bank of the Albert canal between Antwerp and Hasselt. The canal waters would oblige the British to pause before crossing, though he had necessarily to leave a number of bridges undemolished to pass over the few but precious armoured vehicles, guns and trucks returning with the stragglers.

By chance, another German general had halted in the same area where, with energy and skill, he was organising an important and unexpected contribution to the defence force.

Lieutenant-General Kurt Chill was also a senior and older general but one who had been reckoned capable of commanding a field division, the 85th, in France. This formation had been scattered and driven north with the remainder of Seventh Army but, day by day as they marched, Chill had whipped-in whatever he could find of his own men. He had also taken under command pieces of the 84th and 89th Divisions, which accompanied him into Belgium across the Albert Canal. At Turnhout, Chill's headquarters managed to make contact with headquarters of Seventh Army. Instructions were received to march on into the Rhineland where they might reorganise and rest. But while pausing to obtain orders, Chill had discovered that the length of the Albert Canal was undefended except for General Sievers' men. He decided that the Reich would be better served if he stayed in Belgium. On 5th September, he contacted Sievers and agreed to extend the defences towards Maastricht. Meanwhile, he had established strong collecting posts on the bridges round Herentals which identified every German serviceman, vehicle and gun passing over before directing them to a concentration area. As they came in, men and equipment were received by a detachment of Chill's headquarters staff, questioned as to speciality and then allotted to one or another unit of the swelling force.

By such means, the gaps closed on 8th September in the approaches to Holland and north-west Germany. With the arrival of the 176th Division from Aachen, the Albert Canal was manned from Antwerp to Maastricht. Behind this thin screen, the first two parachute regiments were arriving from Germany; one of trainees, the other von der Heydte's 6th Parachute Regiment, the strongest of Student's airborne units, a body of veterans,

55

Above: Colonel-General von Zangen. *Above right:* Lieutenant-General Willi Bittrich. *Right above and below:* SS troops in Holland. *Far right:* The leader of a reconnaissance patrol.

close-knit by comradeship in many past battles.

Every day, almost every hour after the arrival of Horrocks' corps in Brussels, Model had expected to hear that the British Second Army had resumed its advance and broken through into Holland. He did not know that Horrocks' tanks and trucks had petrol only for one hundred miles, a slender ration disposed by Dempsey's decision to leave VIII Corps on the Seine. Horrocks was only too anxious to move on to the Rhine; so much so that, as he tells us with admirable frankness, 'my eyes were entirely on the Rhine, and everything else seemed of subsidiary importance. It never entered my head that the Scheldt would be mined, and that we should not be able to use Antwerp port until the channel had been swept and the Germans cleared from the coast line on either side. Nor did I realise that the Germans would be able to evacuate a large number of the troops trapped in the coastal areas across the mouth of the Scheldt estuary.'

On 6th September, Second Army opened a small forward supply base in Brussels. Dempsey told Horrocks to move on and the 11th Armoured Division attempted at once to cross the Albert Canal. But by this time, Chill's force – now renamed *Kampfgruppe* Chill – had collected a number of anti-tank gun detachments. The crossing was denied with a hot fire which showed that the Germans had put the delay of two days to good use. Horrocks brought forward an infantry division to force a bridgehead at Gheel while the Guards Armoured Division captured another at Beeringen. But now von der Heydte's parachutists came into the battle. Every village, every copse on the heathland round Bourg Leopold was contested as the Guards Armoured Division and Belgian 'White' Brigade fought towards the Meuse-Escaut canal. Then, on the 10th, a chance discovery by an armoured car troop of the British Household Cavalry was turned boldly to advantage. They found an unmapped road which by-passed Hechtel and led forward along this route the tanks of the 3rd Irish Guards to capture, in a waning light, by a brisk action, a bridge across the Meuse-Escaut canal.

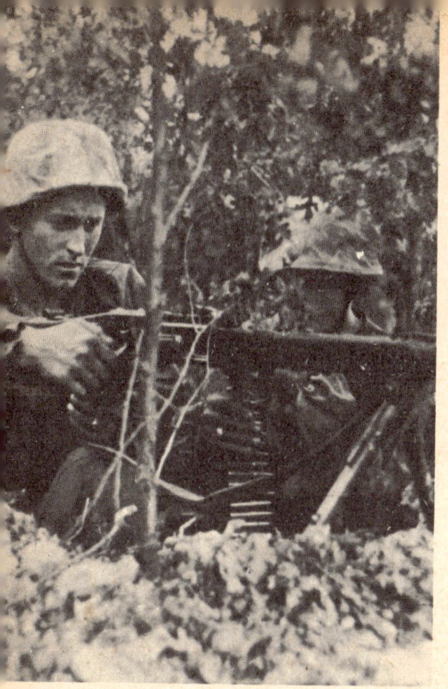

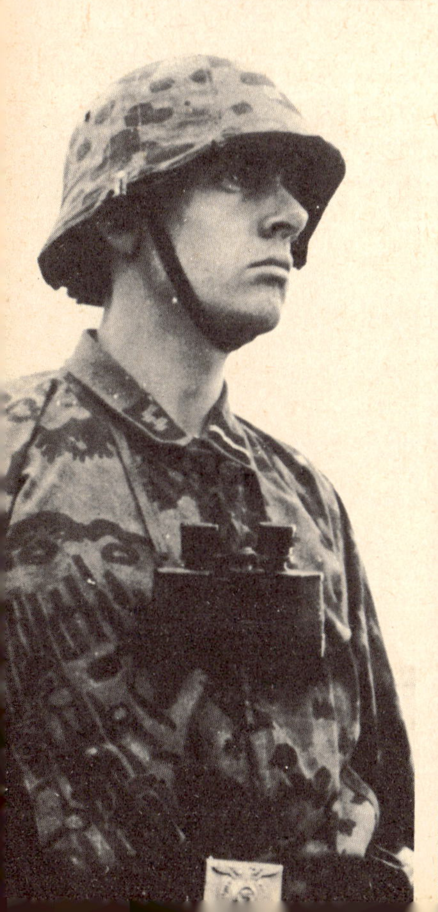

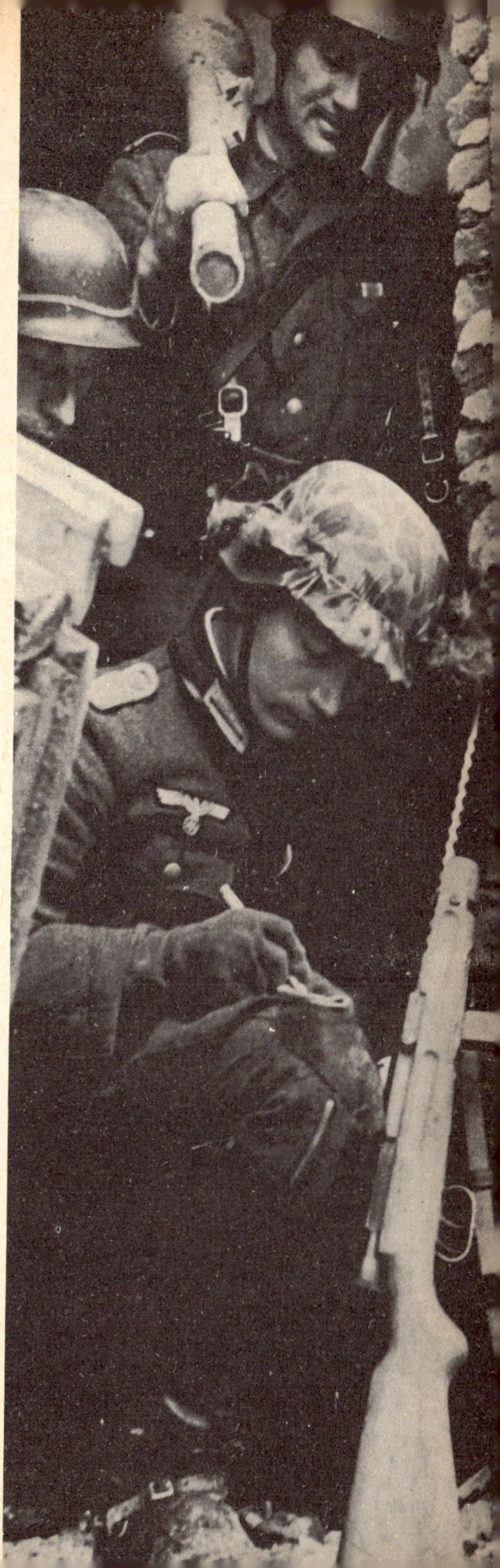

The British now looked over into Holland.

With the capture of a bridgehead over the Meuse-Escaut canal, General Student agreed that the Albert Canal east of Herentals should be abandoned. All troops in this sector were ordered to withdraw during darkness behind the Meuse-Escaut line.

At this time, Model's apprehensions of a strong British advance from Antwerp were diminishing. On the coast, Zangen had been ordered to send eastward whatever troops of Fifteenth Army he could spare from the defence of the Scheldt estuary. The First Parachute Army had several further canals and the rivers Maas, Waal and Rhine on which to deny the approach to Germany through Holland. Behind these, the military commander in Holland had been ordered to improvise further defences. A cause of continuing anxiety was the front in the area of Aachen. Seventh Army were not receiving the reinforcements they needed and there were daily reports of troops massing on the eastern flank of the British Second Army. On the 14th September, Model's Intelligence staff offered a forecast of events in the form of 'orders' which they suggested General Eisenhower might issue.

'The Second British Army . . . will assemble its formations on the Maas-Scheldt and Albert canals. On its right wing it will concentrate an attack force comprised mainly of armoured units which, after forcing a crossing of the Maas, will launch operations to break through into the Rhine – Westphalia (Ruhr) industrial area with the main thrust via Roermond. Covering the northern flank, the left of the (British) Army will close to the Waal at Nijmegen and thereby create the basic conditions necessary to cut off German forces in the Dutch coastal area. In conjunction with these operations, a large-scale airborne landing is planned by the First Allied Airborne Army north of the Lippe river in the area south of Munster, on a date to be decided.'

This was a reasonable guess at allied intentions – Dempsey had considered

British troops prepare to cross the Meuse-Escaut canal

just such a plan – though it committed General Brereton's force to a depth far greater than any airborne operation envisaged by the allies. Both Model and Rundstedt agreed with its general premises, which they now used to endorse their demands for properly formed and equipped divisions from the Reich.

With the approach of the battle line and in expectation of a major thrust across the Rhine south of the Lippe river, Model had already moved his headquarters further into Holland behind the protective covering of the Maas, Waal and Rhine and the intermediate canals. He thus positioned himself outside the northern touch-line of the anticipated field of play while retaining, thanks to the efficiency of German communications, the ability to signal speedily instructions to the principals in his team: Zangen of Fifteenth Army; Student, with the First Parachute Army in the centre; Brandenberger and Seventh Army to the south.

In Holland, the local military commander was an air force general, Friedrich Christiansen. Though despised by his clever, egocentric chief of staff, who referred to him in private as 'the tug-boat skipper', 'cunning as a peasant', he had served the Reich well by maintaining only sufficient pressure on the Dutch to meet his needs without incurring their extreme resentment; an example which his SS colleague would have done well to follow. Ordered by Model to form fighting units from the hotch-potch of training establishments, supply depots and garrison staffs – all that remained after he had despatched Sievers' division and his one corps headquarters to the Albert canal – he acted promptly. Forward, on the Waal and the Rhine, he arranged a screen organisation to catch the scatterings from the defeat in France. To command it, he appointed an aged general, Hans von Tettau, to whom he gave the NCOs School and a 'battalion' formed from the training base of the SS Panzer Grenadiers. Within ten days, these units had intercepted over 3,000 men – sailors, airmen and soldiers of various arms – who were organised into units, the transport and weapons brought in amongst them being divi-

Lieutenant-Colonel Walter Harzer

ded on a roughly equal basis.

Behind the screen, Christiansen's chief of staff disposed the remaining troops between garrisons and a local reserve. From the training establishments of the Waffen-SS, he squeezed two more units: two more and a reconnaissance company came from the Herman Göring Division's recruit training centre; two were found by the military police; three by Georgians and Caucasians who had volunteered from Russian prisoner of war cages to serve in the Wehrmacht; and amongst the dregs was a battalion of Dutch SS, some of whom had been recruited from criminals in local prisons. It was a motley body, ranging from the seasoned officers and NCOs from the schools, some partly incapacitated by wounds, through the raw but devoted SS and Herman Göring recruits, to the *ad hoc* battalions and batteries caught in Tettau's net, descending to the sly and anxious renegades from Russia and Holland.

The allied intelligence at this time of 'small numbers of hastily organised defence units' in the Arnhem area, 'not amounting to more than a brigade at the most' was not inexact. That is to say, it was not inexact as far as it went. What was not known in the first half of September was that Model, denied armour from Germany, had ordered two Panzer divisions in France to concentrate in Holland.

Amongst the wreck of the Panzer army withdrawing through France in late August was a corps containing two divisions of the Waffen-SS: the 9th (*Hohenstaufen*) and 10th (*Frundesberg*). Transferred to Normandy from Poland during June, this corps, II SS Panzer, had arrived in time to join the battle round Caen and owed something to Kluge who had begun their disengagement without Hitler's sanction, thereby preserving some of their strength. Committed again to reopen the Falaise pocket, they succeeded briefly but at a cost in tanks. When Model ordered their withdrawal to the Seine, allied aircraft struck their columns repeatedly. It was a depleted corps that crossed the river north of Paris, yet still an entity. Scarcely pausing, they moved on between the Scheldt and the Sambre, threatened by the onrush of British tanks into Cambrai and the advanced guards of Hodges' army to the east. Changing direction, increasing the pace, General Willi Bittrich, the corps commander, drew away from his pursuers and at last, beyond Maastricht, behind the Maas, found safe territory in which he might rest his weary remnants.

A message from Model reached him here on 4th September: he was to send the two divisions – or what remained of them – to concentration areas north and north-east of Arnhem. Next day, Bittrich was ordered to follow with his headquarters. Behind Arnhem he would reform his corps, retaining one of his own and receiving two other skeleton Panzer divisions to be disengaged as soon as possible from support of the Seventh Army line. At once, accompanied by a staff officer and radio truck, Bittrich drove to Oosterbeek to see Model, while his headquarters packed and made ready to move.

Between the 7th, when Bittrich arrived at Oosterbeek, and the 10th September, when his headquarters had established itself at Doetinchem, east of the Ijssel, there were several changes of plan for II Panzer Korps, not surprisingly in view of the continually changing circumstances of the battlefield. Zangen had now succeeded in reorganising one division of those he had evacuated across the Scheldt, the 245th, which would shortly pass to First Parachute Army, but it was a feeble one. It would be followed by the 59th, two-thirds below strength in infantry but otherwise in good heart. These troops should cover adequately the rear of Sievers' division, the parachutists and *Kampfgruppe* Chill. To the south, Model signalled Rundstedt on the 8th, '... there is only a very thin and totally inadequate defence line. Here the enemy enjoys almost complete freedom of movement as far as the West Wall which is held – to the rear of Seventh Army – by only seven or eight battalions on a front of 120 kilometres (seventy-five miles).' North of Aachen he was organising an *ad hoc* formation, Korps Feldt, named after its commander, with a makeshift division of soldiers and airmen. The frontier district headquarters, *Wehrkreis VI*, would equip Korps Feldt and provide it with whatever odd tanks and guns – mostly from old French stocks – it could scrape together. Once again the hospitals would offer men from the various wards to form 'stomach case' or 'ear case' battalions. 9th SS Panzer Division was to be prepared to move south to assist if the Americans penetrated the West Wall. The 10th was to go back to Germany to refit.

Increasingly, both Model and Rundstedt, his immediate superior as commander-in-chief in the west, began to fear an invasion of Holland from the sea; German Intelligence had reported that assault landing craft were being assembled once more by the allies. Such landings might well be in combination with an airborne assault. As commander in the Netherlands, General Christiansen was ordered to consider plans to counter such operations. With the initiative in his enemies' hands, and indications of fresh dangers each day from intelligence and operational reports, Model was obliged to diversify his arrangements. On 10th September, when Hitler's headquarters ordered the early despatch to Germany of one of the two SS Panzer divisions, there was a further change: it was the 9th (*Hohenstaufen*) that was now to go

General Friedrich Christiansen, military governor of Holland

since the 10th had been strengthened by fragments of two panzer battalions directed into its area.

In the absence of the divisional commander, lying wounded in hospital, the 9th Division was commanded by its chief of staff, the young and capable Walter Harzer. He was ordered by Bittrich to pass all his armour – about fifteen Mark IV and V tanks – armoured and scout cars, half-tracked armoured infantry carriers, artillery, mortars and supply trucks to Major-General Heinz Harmel's 10th Division. Troop carrying and supply transport was to be handed over progressively

Major-General Heinz Harmel, commander 10th SS Panzer Division

as the 9th left by rail for Germany, the first trains being scheduled to depart on 13th September.

The presence of II SS Panzer Korps had not gone unnoticed by the local members of the brave Dutch underground movement. To avoid as far as possible detection by the radio-direction finding apparatus of the German counter-intelligence organisation, local messages were collected by individual groups and then sent to an area radio transmitter for despatch to London. Late on 8th September, the leader of the 'Albrecht' group collected a message from Roermond reporting: 'Large transports of SS Panzer troops have passed through here from Maastricht direction (during the night 7th/8th) heading northwards towards Maas and Waal.' This was either 10th SS Panzer or part of corps headquarters. On the 14th, 'Albrecht' group reported again, noting the presence of a division (actually both the 9th and 10th) west and east of the river Ijssel and a headquarters (actually II SS Panzer Korps) at Doetinchem. On the same day, the Rotterdam radio also passed to London a message from the 'Kees' group: 'SS Division *Hohenstrufl (Hohenstaufen)* along Ijssel. Units from this division noticed from Arnhem to Zutphen-Appeldoorn. HQ perhaps at Eefde (actually in Beekbergen). Field fortifications being built along the Ijssel.'

These details were passed urgently to SHAEF. Combing through their card-index system, Eisenhower's Intelligence staff had no difficulty in identifying the subject of the Dutch messages as 9th SS Panzer, with which might well be found the 10th. It was expected that they would be re-equipped with tanks from a Panzer reserve park believed to be 'in the area of Cleves (Kleve)' just across the Rhine in Westphalia.

General Eisenhower's chief-of-staff, Bedell Smith, was understandably alarmed at this new and more detailed corroboration of 'Albrecht's' report from Roermond. His chief agreed that he should go forward to see Field-Marshal Montgomery to discuss whether they should either drop the equivalent of a second division at Arnhem or move the 101 or 82nd to drop with the British 1st Division.

General Bedell Smith recalled after the war that his mission was not taken seriously by the Field-Marshal who 'ridiculed the idea' and 'waved my objections airily aside'. Yet, valid as these impressions may be, strong reasons prompted Montgomery to dismiss any idea of a change of plan – and hence a postponement – at such a late hour. Every day there were intelligence reports, many from underground sources, of new and unexpected enemy troop concentrations. The majority of these proved to be misleading. Though the reports of armour at Arnhem certainly had some substance – allied air reconnaissance had photographed a small number of tanks in the area after the first Dutch reports had come in – they did not indicate strength. Everywhere along the front there were small groups of tanks, sometimes with self-propelled guns. There were also various Panzer 'divisions', but these were known to be skeletons of the original bodies. The British and American armies had passed in their pursuit across France column after column of broken and burned out tanks and other vehicles; manifest testimony of the destruction of the German Panzer army in the west. Why should they now believe that the 'tanks' and 'Panzer divisions' at Arnhem were numerous and threatening when elsewhere it was known that they were not? Moreover, if they delayed Market to change the plan, were they not giving the Germans yet more time to recover their strength?

All operations of war involved a risk. It was reckoned by the Field-Marshal that they had calculated this risk as far as it was possible to do so. Given the weather, Operation Market was on.

Army, Air Force and SS tried to recruit Dutch into 'local' defence units. Very few responded but the variety of uniforms reflects the several controlling agencies

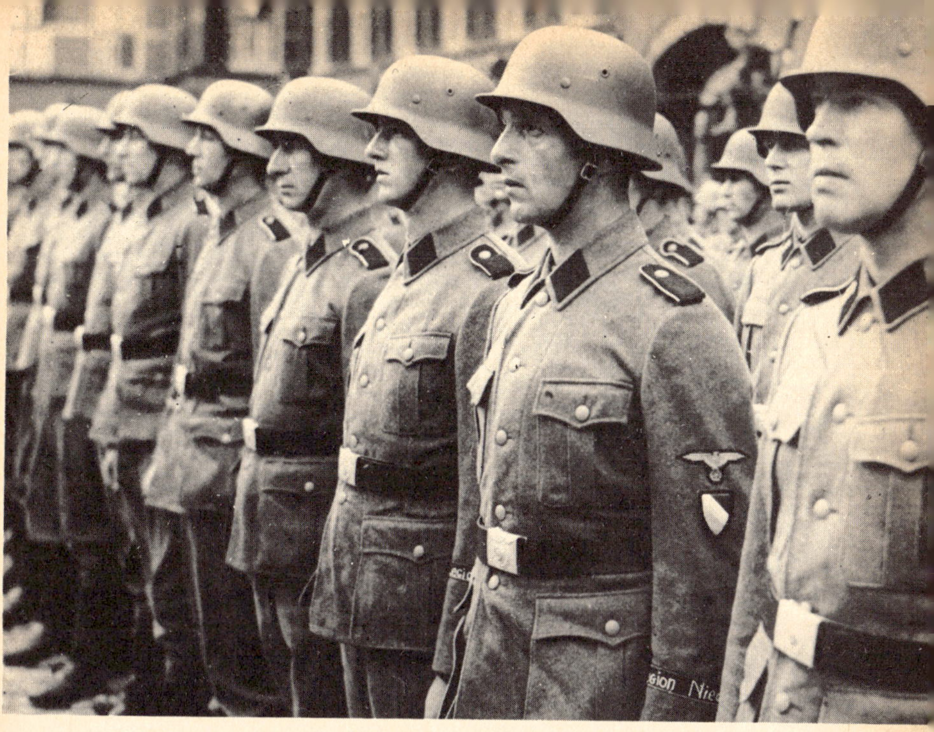

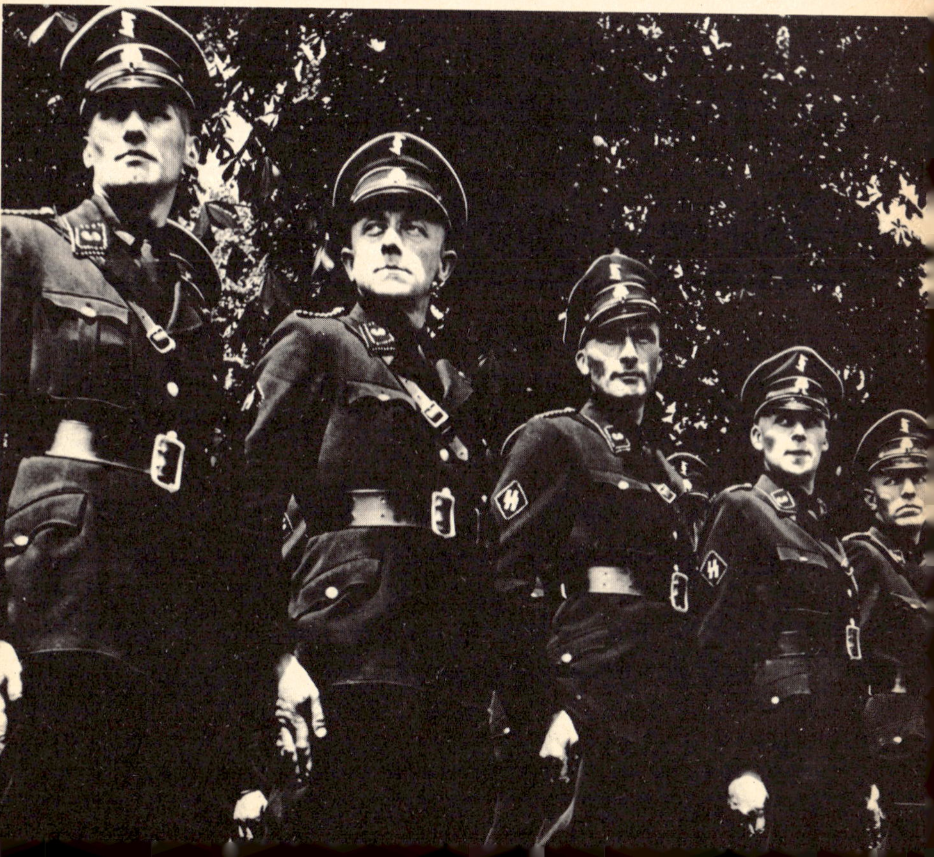

Model (left) confers with Student, Bittrich and Harmel

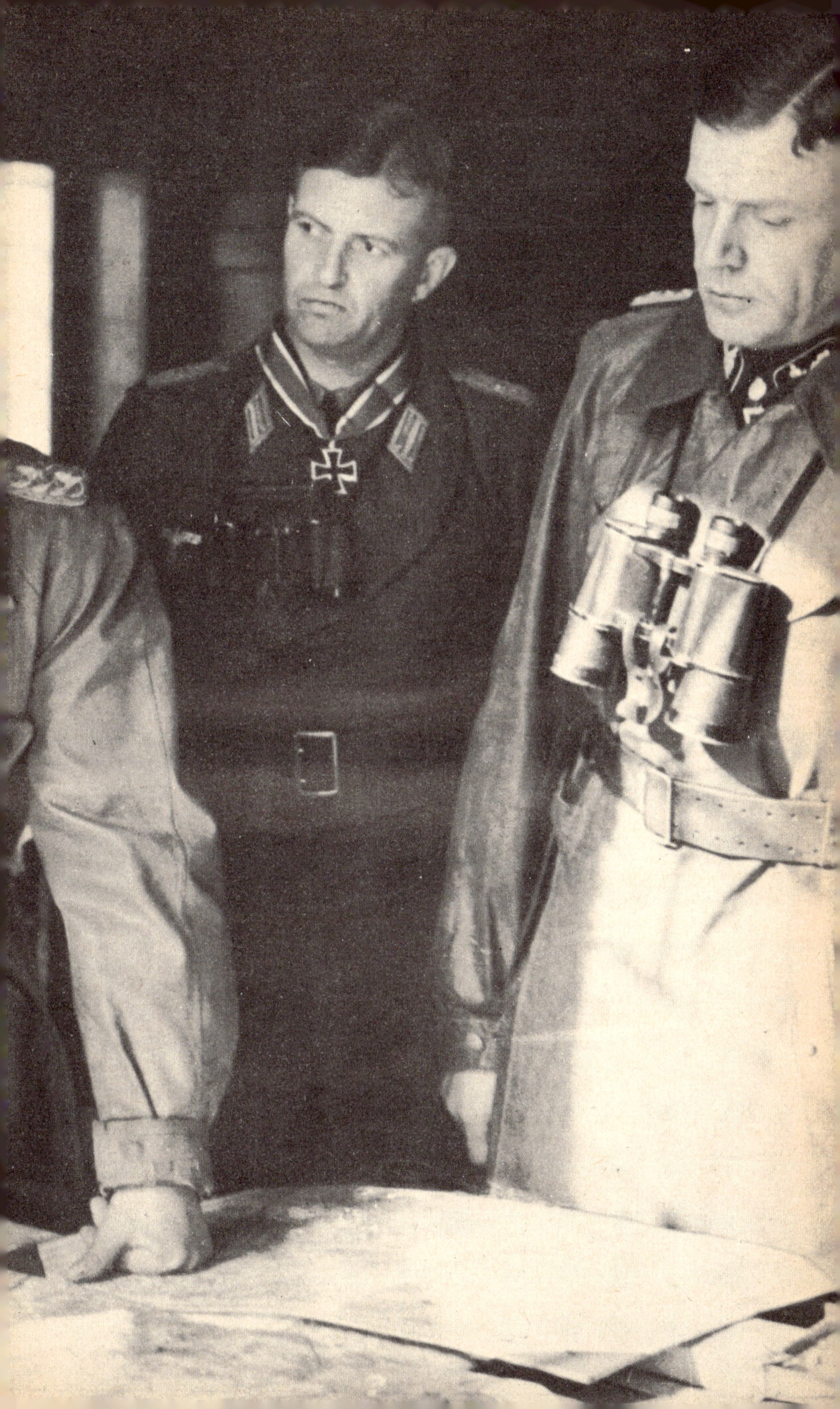

16th September

The Reichskommisar controlling Holland was a general of the SS, Hans Albin Rauter. He was nominally the servant of several German departments of state but the only one of significance was the SS and police department under the notorious Heinrich Himmler. On the instructions of his chief, Rauter called on Model at his headquarters in the Tafelberg Hotel in Oosterbeek on 15th September as a courtesy and to discuss the operational situation from their respective standpoints.

It was Rauter's task to maintain internal order. He half expected a rising by the Dutch people at any time and had advised General Christiansen to ensure that military headquarters were properly protected against surprise attack. During his visit, he now asked Model whether he had sufficient troops to secure the command post of Army Group B in case of insurrection. Model, and his chief of staff Krebs, found this amusing. 'We have more than we need,' said Krebs, '250 military police look after our security.'

Rauter persisted. Supposing there should be an airborne landing; would this force still be enough?

The two soldiers now gave Rauter a brief discourse on the use of parachute troops. Their selection and training are of a special nature, they explained; therefore they are used only at critical times. Nijmegen and Arnhem are unlikely to become the centre of a critical battle. The supply line of the British Second Army runs from Cherbourg (so they believed) and must therefore be stretched to its maximum extent. Antwerp is not open to their use and will continue to be denied even after the Scheldt is cleared as it lies within range of the V1 launchers. Arnhem was more than ninety miles from the British line. 'Surely you know,' said Model 'that Montgomery is a very cautious general, not inclined to plunge into mad adventures.' Would he attempt to rush forward over such a distance and without a forward supply base? It was their view that the allied airborne army would be used near Düsseldorf when their ground forces had crossed the Rhine. Faced with such a professional opinion, Rauter offered no further argument.

Hans Albin Rauter   Reichskommissar SS for Holland

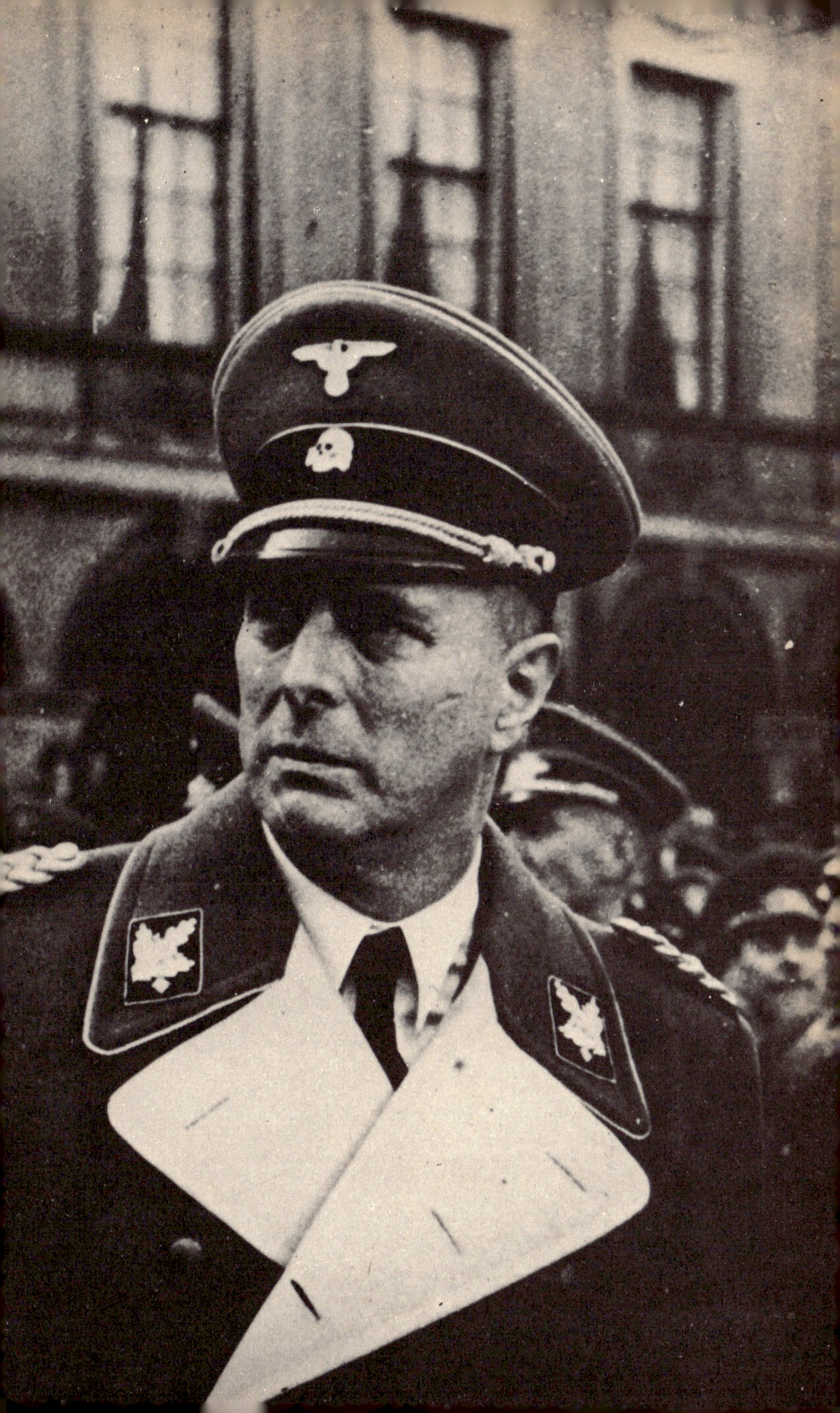

All the same, he was not convinced. The British were a sporting nation, always ready for a gamble, he felt. That day he gave orders to Major Sepp Krafft, commanding one of the Waffen-SS recruit 'battalions' to move on the 16th September to Oosterbeek to be at. hand if Headquarters, Army Group B should be attacked.

On 16th September, Student's operational report concluded that '... increased motor transport activity and confirmed armoured preparations (by XXX Corps) strengthen the appreciation ... that a heavy attack must be expected shortly.'

That day, the dispirited 245th Division from the Scheldt arrived in rear of *Kampfgruppe* Chill and began to dig defences along the edges of the drainage ditches and the canal banks, amongst the thin leafy spinneys and the villages. To the west, General Poppe brought his 59th Division to the railway and began to load guns and trucks on to flat cars for the journey into North Brabant.

North of Arnhem, Lieutenant-Colonel Walter Hartzer remained with the bulk of the 9th Division; for only a small proportion of his command had left for Germany due to the raids of allied bombers and the Dutch underground on the railway tracks and until the last he had been ordered to preserve the capability to fight. He possessed still the greater part of his tank company and almost all of his other fighting vehicles. To account for this failure to comply with orders he had told corps headquarters and 10th Division that what remained was unserviceable and could not be moved until his fitters had done their work, a lie made plausible by the gratuitous removal of tank tracks and truck wheels and the genuine bustle of exhaustive repair and maintenance in all parks in his area. None of his equipment had been seen by allied airmen or reconnaissance cameras because of extensive screening by camouflage nets.

He reckoned without the watchful Dutch underground.

On 16th September, Rotterdam transmitted another message from the 'Kees' group. 'At Arnhem (there is a sign) *Meldekopf Hohenstauff* – Hohenstaufen Division Information Post.

Above: Park Hotel, Hartenstein, Model's headquarters. *Right:* Dutch resistance radio

This is assembly place of members of the SS division previously reported. Also at Arnhem, *Meldekopf Hartzer* presumably forming part of a unit situated south of Arnhem.'

Neither this nor any other of the connected underground messages were passed to General Browning. Indirectly, through an officer at headquarters of XXX Corps, he learned that there were reports of German armour in Arnhem and he recalled a similar report in connection with Operation Comet. When he queried this with 21st Army Group, the reply was meant to be both accurate and reassuring: 'not more than a battle group, if that.'

Reviewing in his mind what he possessed in anti-tank weapons loaded into gliders and under the parachutists' aircraft, Browning reflected that one armoured battle group was the most that the corps could cope with. But it was too late to draw back.

On the 16th September, General Brereton lunched with Browning in the club house at Moor Park and wished him luck. His British deputy was 'in good spirits', he noted in his diary. Everything now depended on the final weather forecast. At 1900 hours, assured of a fine day in spite of early morning fog, Brereton made his decision: they would fly the operation.

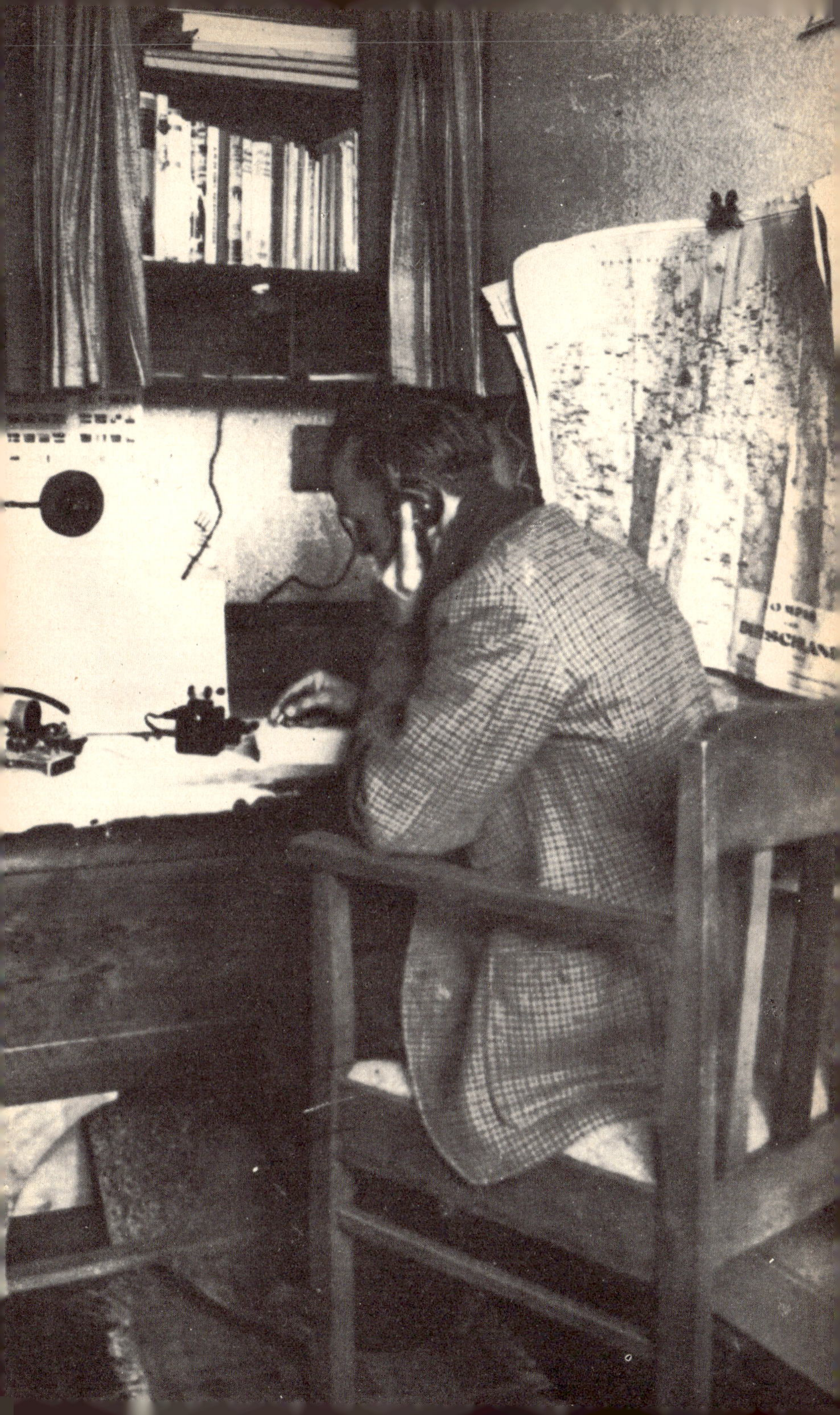

Market begins

As it grew dark on the Saturday night, while the parachutists and the glider troops made their way to the airfield canteens, 200 Lancasters of Royal Air Force Bomber Command and twenty-three Mosquitoes began their journey towards the four German airfields supporting the Netherlands and one near Berlin. The latter, Rheine, was the subject of a special operation designed to crater the runways and thus deny take-off facility to the new jet fighters stationed there, the first in Luftwaffe service. Ahead of the bomber force flew a combined force of American and British aircraft containing radio devices to jam the enemy radar detectors.

While these raids proceeded, fifty-nine RAF bombers struck flak defences in the Netherlands. The targets had been carefully selected so as not to suggest to the Luftwaffe intelligence staffs that air corridors were being opened.

Next morning, bombers continued their preparatory work. Under Spitfire escort, 100 RAF bombers struck at flak defences on Walcheren and Schouwen islands and flak ships nearby. Later, a huge force of more than 1,000 bombers and fighter escorts of the United States Eighth Air Force strafed 112 anti-aircraft positions. By this time, the last tendrils of morning fog had dispersed from British airfields and the air transports had risen up from the fields in Hampshire, Berkshire, Wiltshire, Oxfordshire and Gloucestershire, Lincolnshire, Northamptonshire and Cambridgeshire, 'like a great swarm of bees ascending, singing and droning' as they appeared to an old farmer near Hertford. In the ground dispersals, 1,131 allied fighter pilots waited in their Spitfires, Tempests, Mosquitoes, P-47s, P-38s and P-51s, ready for the signal to spring into the air to protect the soldiers of the allied airborne army *en route* to the Netherlands. Coastal beacons stood ready with searchlights and radio to provide ground fixes for the navigators. Two beacon ships were at their sea rendezvous while over a range of the North Sea narrows air-sea rescue teams watched the skies, listened to their radios.

The Pathfinders led the transports:

'Gathering in all the little chickens'
C47 Dakotas in flight

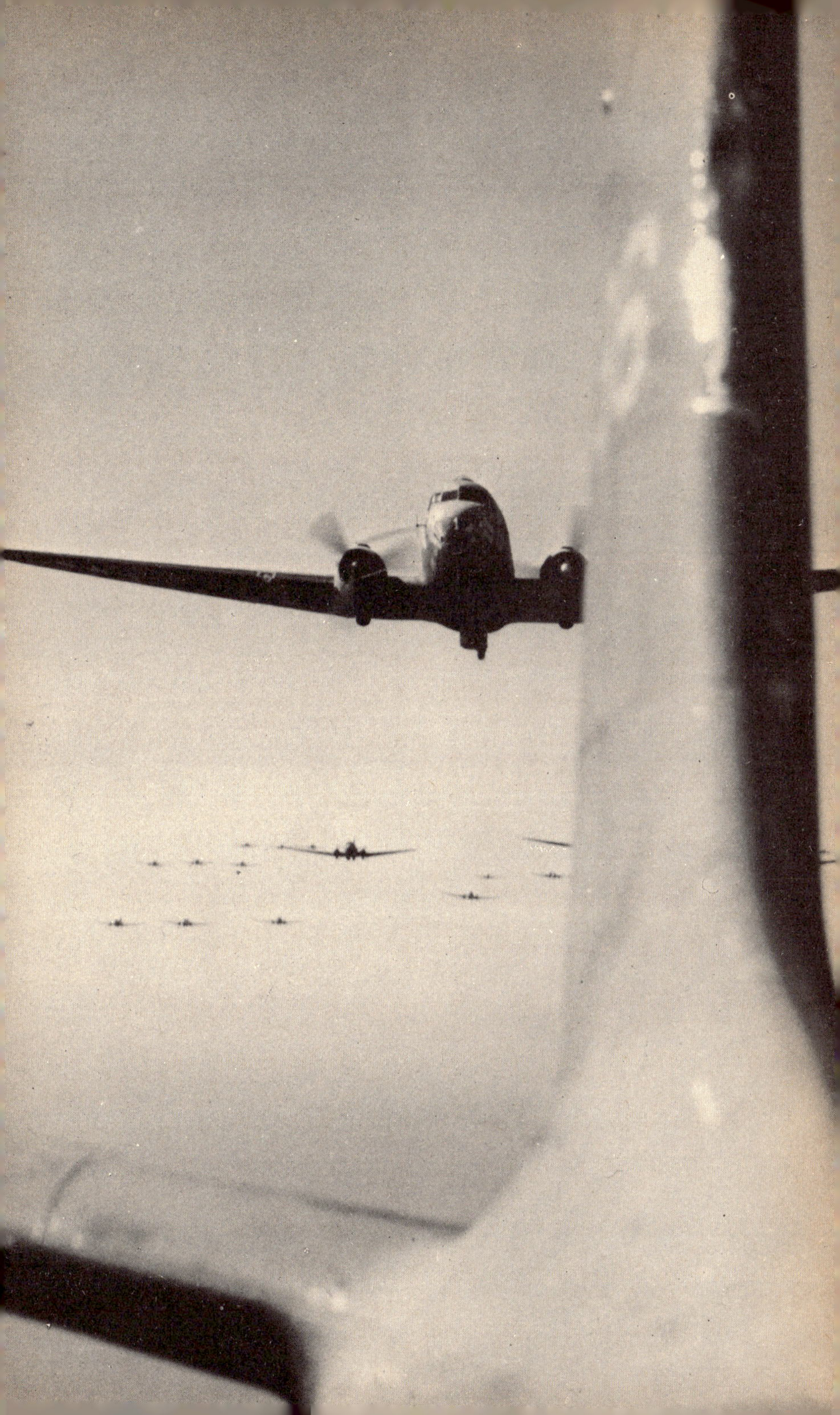

Loaded for battle, Horsa gliders form up for their tugs

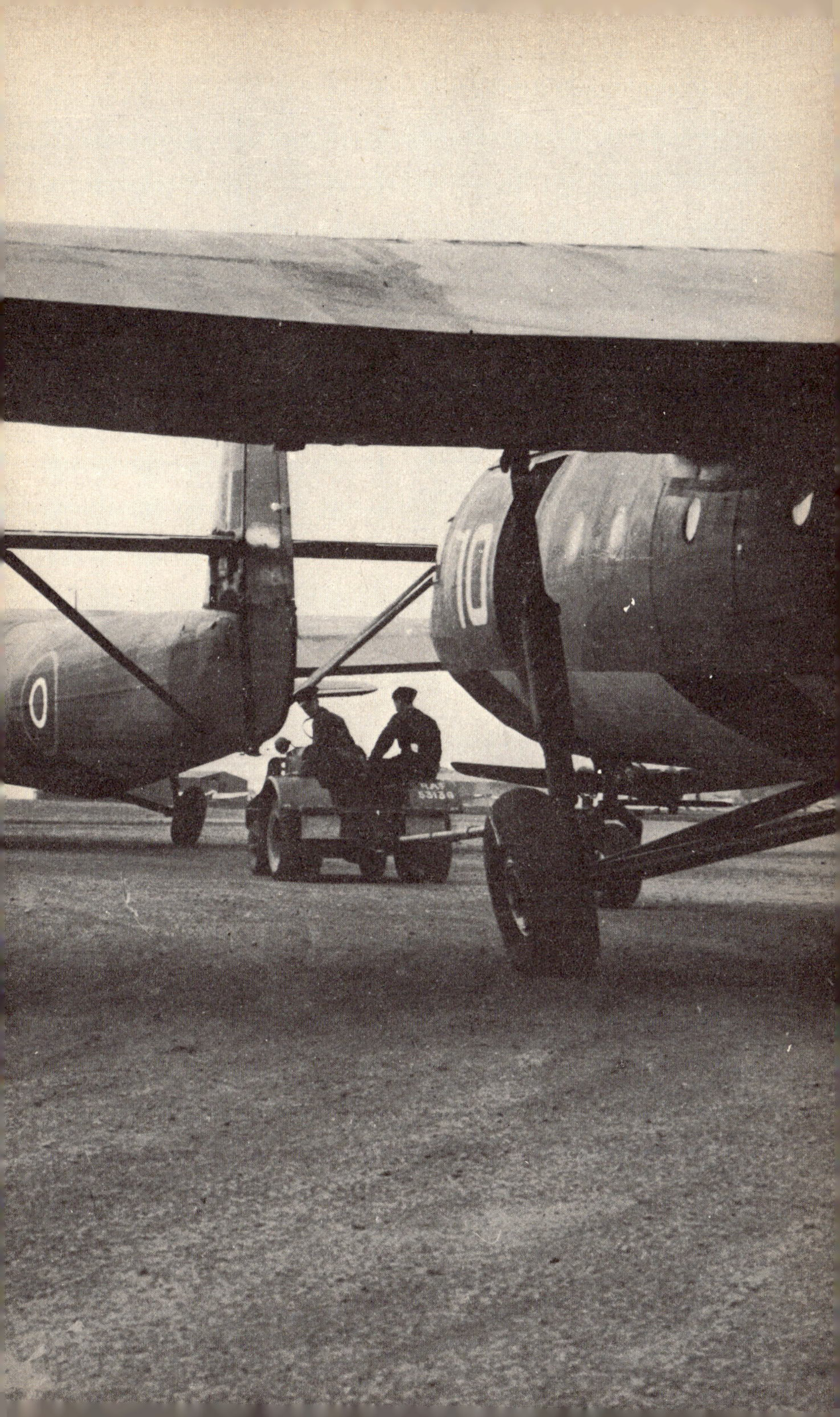

twelve converted British bombers, six American Dakotas, each with aircrews selected for their skill in navigation and dropping accuracy, each with teams of the army pathfinder units who would have twenty minutes to lay out their coloured marker panels and radio beacons on the glider landing zones, the parachute dropping zones. Those carried in the British bombers suffered the disadvantage of a journey spent in almost complete darkness in the tunnel of the hull. They were unable to smoke due to the fire risk and when the time came to make their exits, they would have to leave through an aperture in the floor. In contrast, the Dakota offered bucket seats, a warm cabin with windows and a spacious door in rear on the port side from which to jump. Smoking was permitted. There were no volunteers for transportation in the bombers.

Travelling with the main stream was Ed Murrow, correspondent of the Columbia Broadcasting System who recorded his impressions:

'Early this morning, the paratroopers, laden down with equipment, walked out across a green field and climbed into the C-47s. After we took off we seemed to gather more ships as we passed a series of airfields and the pilot said: "We're gathering in all the little chickens before we cross the big water." The paratroops sat relaxed; two of them were asleep. The door at the rear of the plane had been removed; all the belts and hinges had been covered with tape to prevent the parachute harness from fouling. The big fellow near the door looked down and said: "Look at them land girls down there picking potatoes!" The men were completely relaxed. Occasionally, one would rub the palm of his hand on his trouser leg. One sat staring into his tin helmet . . .

'Now we are over Holland and I'm going to move forward, up to the pilot's compartment, and I've got my parachute harness hung on the door. We're flying over country that has been inundated . . .

'The skipper is sitting there very

Left: Inside a C47, a para holds his reserve parachute and 'walkie-talkie'.
Far right: 'There they go . . .'

calmly, flying with one hand. There is no traffic on this one railway (track being followed), which stands well above the water. It seems to have been built along the top of a dyke. The countryside below looks like the area round the Mississippi during the flood time except that all the houses seem to be covered with red tile. The spire of a magnificent old Dutch church rises clear above the little houses that surround it. One barge in a canal, but completely deserted.

'I'm standing here, looking back down the length of the ship now. The crew chief is on his knees back in the very rear, talking into his intercom ... They're looking out of the window rather curiously, almost as if they were passengers on a peacetime airline ...

'The pilot of this plane has just said: "Jerry must not live here any more. He isn't shooting at us." We've been flying straight into Holland for something like twenty minutes, so far without any opposition. Our fighters are down, just almost nosing along the hedgerows, searching the little villages, and are up above us and on both sides. This is the real meaning of air power.

'There's a burst of flak. You can see it right from the side. It's coming from the port side just across our nose, but a little bit low. Tracers going across us, in front of our nose. I think it's coming from that little village just beside the canal. More tracer coming up now, a lovely orange colour it is, in just about forty seconds now our ship will drop the men; they will walk out on to Dutch soil. You can probably hear the snap as they check the lashing on the static line (anchored in the aircraft). There they go! Do you hear them count? Three ... four ... five ... six ... seven ... eight ... nine ... ten ... eleven ... twelve ... thirteen ... fourteen ... fifteen ... sixteen. Now every man is out. I can see their 'chutes going down now. Every man clear ... they're dropping beside the little windmill near a church, hanging there very gracefully, and seem to be completely relaxed, like nothing so much as khaki dolls hanging beneath green lampshades. I see the men go down just north of a little road. The whole sky is filled with parachutes.

They're all going down so slowly.'

It was 12 30 hours.

At Vught, a pleasant town on the Dommel river, General Student had his headquarters. 'At about noon (1300 hours British Summer Time)', he says, 'I was disturbed at my desk by a roaring in the air of such mounting intensity that I finally left my study and went on to the balcony. Wherever I looked, I saw aircraft, troop carriers and large (bomber) aircraft towing gliders. They flew both in formation and singly. It was an immense stream which passed quite low over the house. I was greatly impressed by the spectacle and I must confess that during these minutes the danger of the situation never occurred to me. I merely recalled with some regret my own earlier airborne operations.' Turning to his chief-of-staff who had come out to join him on the balcony, he cried, 'Oh, how I wish that I had ever had such powerful means at my disposal!' Then, recovering, he began to call for reports concerning those who had landed close by (101st), and the destination of the greater (northern) stream which had passed on.

A most complete answer came to him far more quickly than he could have expected. One of the gliders he had seen had subsequently been hit by flak, losing part of a wing. It faltered and then hurtled to the ground, killing instantaneously the American soldiers and crew inside. A platoon of German soldiers ran to the wreckage and began to search the bodies. In the breast pocket of an officer, a soldier named Koch found a file of papers and maps which, after a moment's glance, he passed to his sergeant. It was a copy of the plan for Operation Market.

This plan was on Student's desk within a few hours. It told him not only where the landings had taken place but precisely who had arrived, who was to follow and what tasks each airborne unit had been given. While the information and consequent orders were prepared for the formations of First Parachute Army, an attempt was made urgently to contact Model's headquarters in the Tafelberg Hotel at Oosterbeek. But it seemed that the premises had been abandoned.

At 1300 hours, the commander of Army Group B had been drinking a glass of wine prior to lunch, for which a cold table had already been set out. Close to the hour, the sound of many aircraft engines was heard – not for the first time that day as there had been several air raids. 'Bombers,' said an officer, going to the window to look out. What he saw alarmed him much more: enemy parachutists were dropping in the open country immediately to the west.

This was formidable news. All the officers present had heard of the surprise capture by the British of several high headquarters in their advance across France and there had been some talk of what should be done when such circumstances threatened. Whatever their immediate reactions, now that they were in precisely this danger, however, outward calm was preserved due to Model's presence. Quickly, he detailed three tasks: the evacuation of the area to General Bittrich's location; their movement to be covered by Sepp Krafft's SS Training Battalion; Generals Bittrich and Christiansen to be ordered to send troops forward as quickly as possible. This delivered, Model ran upstairs to pack a suitcase and such papers as were immediately to hand. Throwing on a black leather jacket, he hurried downstairs, carrying his case past the scampering headquarters staff. At the entrance way, the Commander-in-Chief's case sprang open releasing clothes and toilet articles on to the paving. These were bundled roughly back while his staff car stood waiting, the engine running, the driver nervously hooting though no one stood in their way. His suitcase loaded, Model leapt into the front seat, his personal staff into the back and the car accelerated on to the road, followed by a column of other cars, radio vehicles and trucks.

A mile along the road towards Arnhem, Model saw an SS major pedalling a bicycle hard in the same direction. The staff car pulled alongside. Leaning over the open window, Model called out, 'Which way to General Bittrich's headquarters?'

'The Doetinchem road,' the major shouted back. With a roar, the staff car shot on into Arnhem.

Horsa in free flight

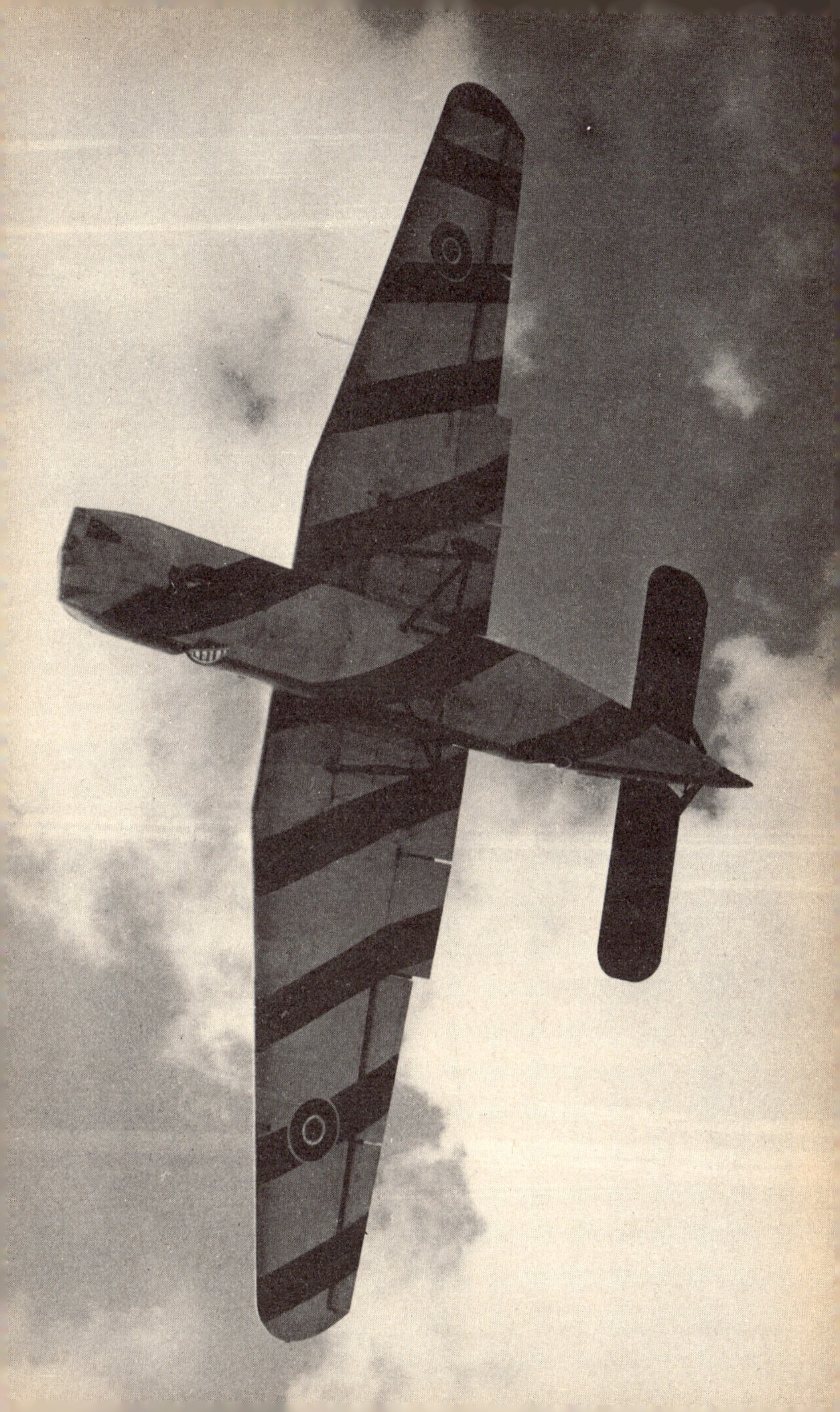

British bomber converted for paratroops

In the town, the Commander-in-Chief stopped at the garrison headquarters. Inside, it was clear that they had had the news of the landings; for everywhere there was confusion: staff officers, clerks, orderlies and police were running about, the officers and NCOs shouting, telephones ringing. Using his powerful voice, Model ordered everyone to be silent and stand still, an order which was instantly obeyed. He then instructed General Kussin, the commander, to send a radio message direct to Hitler, telling him what had happened. The account he gave Kussin included the remark that he had escaped 'through the eye of a needle', a nice phrase which the garrison commander passed on to the Führer.

All this took about five minutes. Model returned to his car and resumed the journey to Doetinchem and General Bittrich's headquarters.

Bittrich did not receive the news that parachutists had landed from Army Group B but from the Luftwaffe Communications Network. Though the pathfinder landings went unnoticed, five minutes after the first release of the main body of parachutists, II SS Panzer Korps had a warning with rough locations of the drop. Soon after, there came a second and more detailed report. It was confirmed that both Arnhem and Nijmegen were involved; areas to which the British Second Army must now drive if they were to effect relief. He issued the following orders before 1330 hours.

'9th SS Panzer Division:
1. Division to reconnoitre in the direction of Arnhem and Nijmegen.
2. The division to go immediately into action, occupying the Arnhem area and destroying the enemy forces which have landed to the west of Arnhem at Oosterbeek. Immediate attack is essential. The aim is to occupy and firmly hold the bridge at Arnhem.'

'10th SS Panzer Division:
Division to proceed immediately to Nijmegen, occupying the main bridge in strength, and defending the bridgeheads (to the south of the River Waal).

'Traffic over the Rhine bridge at Arnhem to be controlled by the Field Security Police of II SS Panzer Korps.'

When Model arrived, he approved all that had been done. Already, 10th SS Panzer Division were calling their men in from the Sunday holiday. They awaited similar confimation from the 9th.

At that time, Harzer was visiting his reconnaissance battalion to decorate its commanding officer with the Iron Cross, an award he had won for gallantry in Normandy. He had seen parachutists and gliders landing at a distance but, strangely, took no action to inform himself of what was happening. If he was relying on the telephone, he overlooked the fact that the Dutch operators were hastening slowly, a policy they often used against the Germans. Eventually, while he was still at lunch with the officers of the battalion, a sweating orderly rode up on a bicycle with the message containing his orders. Now Harzer reacted swiftly.

'By the time I returned to my headquarters at Beekbergen,' Harzer wrote in his battle report, 'my staff had alerted all stand-by units and these reported within an hour that they were ready to move, except the reconnaissance battalion . . . which had to fit tracks on their armoured personnel carriers and mount part of their armament, since these vehicles had been reported unserviceable to corps in order to avoid handing them over to the 10th SS Panzer Division.' There were also stores to be brought back and unloaded from the three railway trains which had left the station for Germany that morning. They were halted and brought back to the nearest open sidings. In all, Harzer still had about 3,500 officers and men left in the area; the 10th Division, 5,000, though Harmel himself was away in Germany.

Between 1600 and 1700 hours that afternoon, written orders arrived at each divisional headquarters, modifying those issued earlier but maintaining the basic idea that the 9th should operate in the Arnhem-Oosterbeek area, the 10th round Nijmegen. Both formations had despatched advanced parties and the reconnaissance battalion of the 9th had already crossed the Rhine to Nijmegen. The 10th were hampered by their lack of radio sets – another item of equipment which Harzer had omitted to transfer – but expected to send off a battle group shortly. Bittrich's staff reminded them that speed of action was essential. Confident as he was that they would contain and then destroy the airborne force on his own side of the Rhine, Bittrich was anxious to do so as far west of Arnhem as possible. Until Harzer arrived or unless Christiansen had acted very promptly indeed, the only force to oppose a move into Arnhem was Sepp Krafft's SS trainees.

After the donning of heavy kit and parachutes, the clambering into the plane; after the aircraft is loaded, the cramped bodies and the engine noise; after the stand-up and the hook-up and the check, the red light and the green light, the rush through the door.

Above their dropping zones, the parachutists passed in quick succession through the doors and apertures, were tossed weightless in the slipstream, heard the exhaust roar die to a murmur, the friendly protest of the canopy opening. One by one, hanging below the sailing silk or nylon, they floated down quietly. The ground swayed and tilted, seemed suddenly to rush up to meet their hanging feet and buffet their bodies.

Few men fouled buildings or trees, few were injured on landing. The majority of the early casualties were killed or wounded during the last stage of the fly-in over the three sets of dropping and landing zones. Four men

Dakota over flooded Dutch country

standing in the door – the leaders of their 'sticks' – were hit by anti-aircraft shrapnel or machine gun bullets. Thirty-five aircraft were lost, some crashing after they had discharged their loads or cast off their tugs. Over the DZs of the 101st, two soldiers drifting down in their parachutes had the horrible experience of being cut to pieces by a C-47 out of control which crashed with them to the ground. The parachute of a soldier in the 82nd failed to open. Five gliders broke loose or were hit by flak and crashed. The air-sea rescue patrol boats recovered a number of their comrades from the North Sea, twice under the fire of the German coastal defences. But despite the fears that flak might destroy up to thirty per cent of the transport force, the great majority of units arrived safely. As expected by the soldiers, aircraft hit and sometimes on fire were flown steadily on by the aircrew without regard for their own subsequent chances of escape.

Near Arnhem, Lieutenant-Colonel 'Sheriff' Thompson, commander of the British airborne artillery battalion, was absorbed in watching the inundations spreading inland from the mouth of the Scheldt when, 'quite suddenly, the air photographs we had so carefully studied came to life and we were fast approaching our landing zone.'

Glider pilot's view

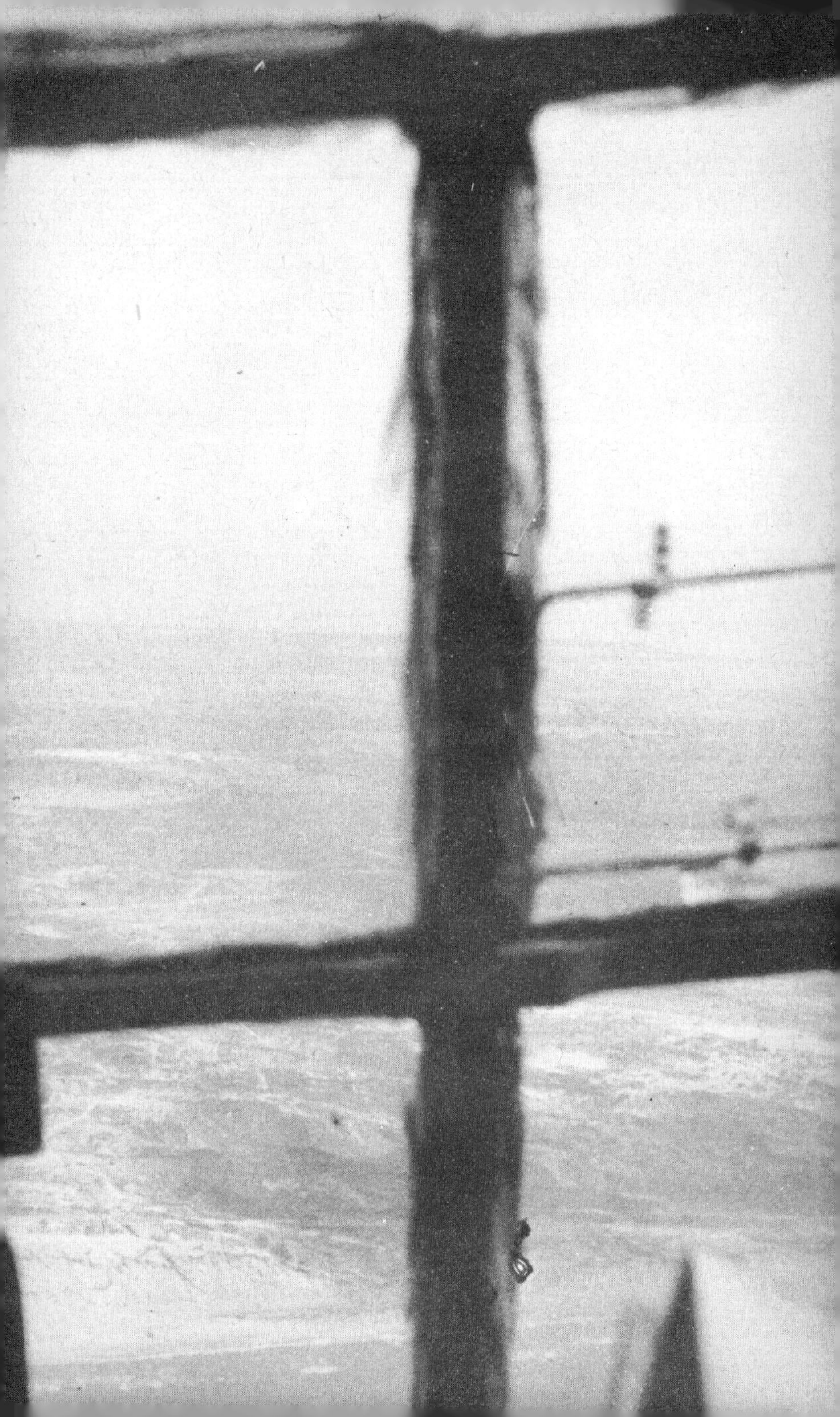

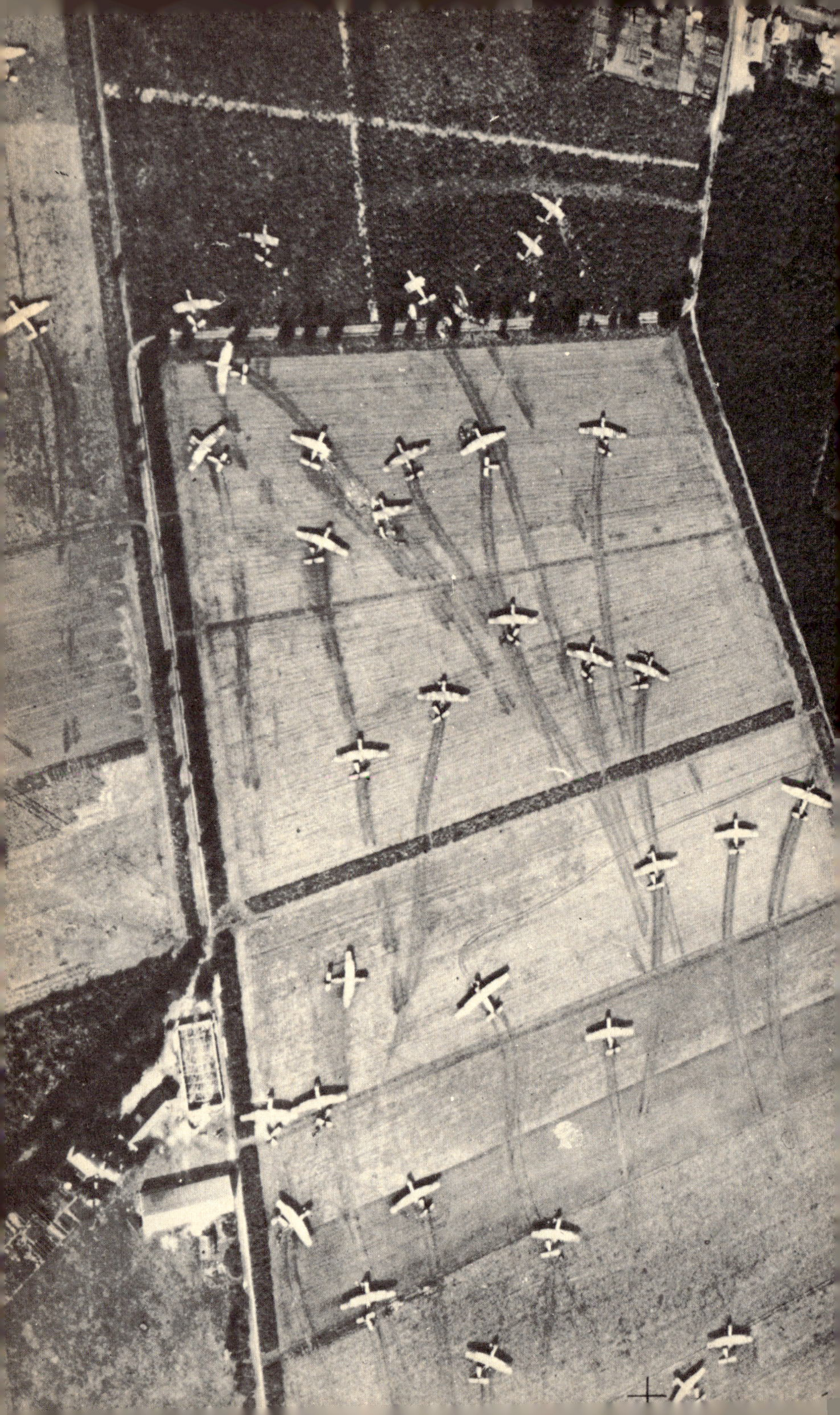

Left: The Air-landing Brigade's gliders just after arrival. *Above:* 'Sherriff' Thompson and his artillery HQ unload from their gliders. *Below:* Lieutenant-Colonel John Frost (right)

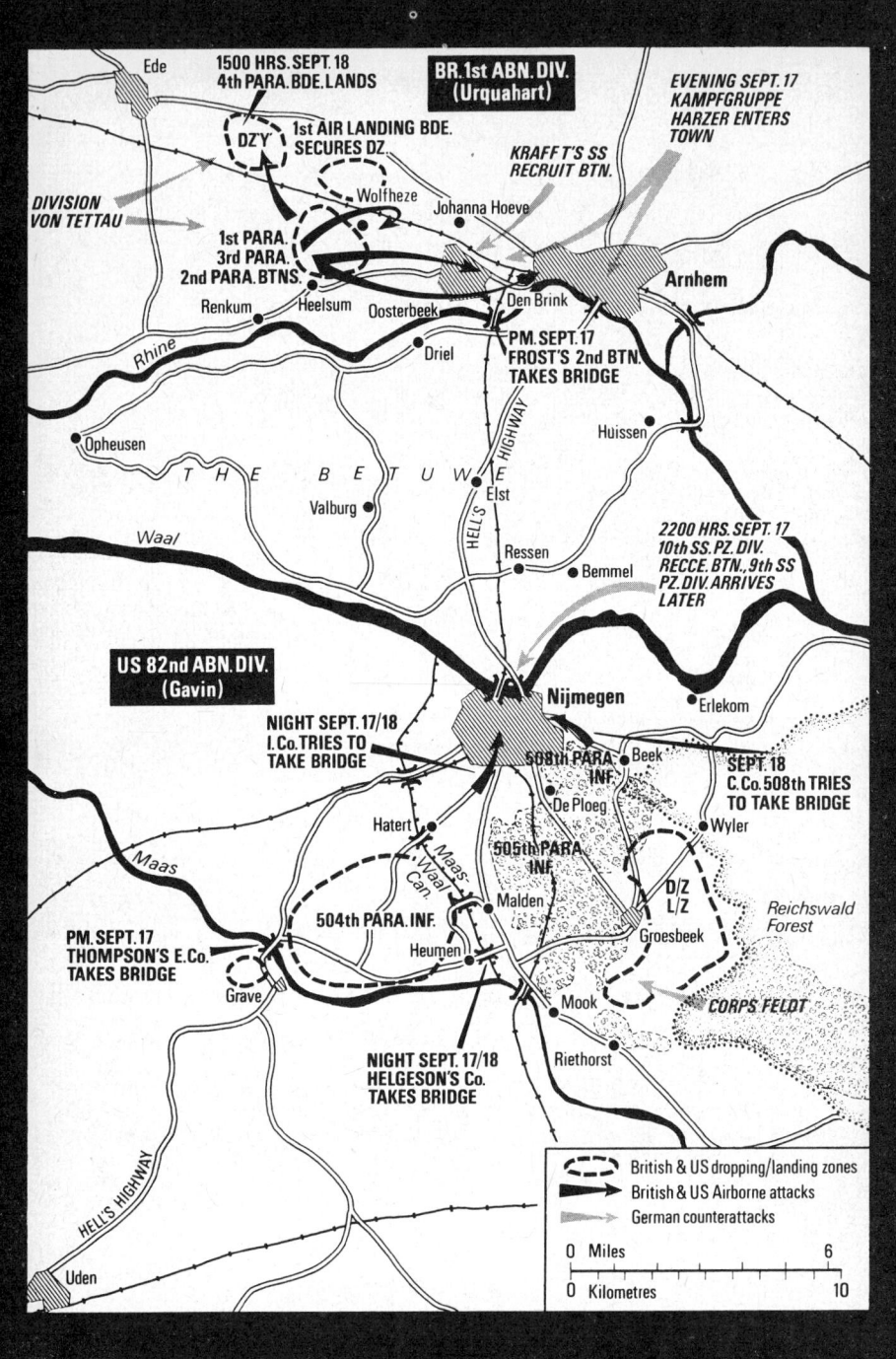

The situation in the US 82nd and British 6th Airborne Divisions' areas on 17th/18th September

Major Wilson's British pathfinder company had done their work well. All dropping and landing zones were marked and the British and American navigators brought their pilots to the sight of the release points. 149 Dakotas of IX Troop Carrier Command dropped Brigadier Lathbury's 1st Parachute Brigade on DZ 'X' while 38 and 46 Groups cast off 291 gliders for LZ 'S' and 'Z'. Inside the Horsas and the giant Hamilcars, free now to skim silently to their destinations, were Urquhart, divisional headquarters, much of the airborne reconnaissance squadron and the 1st Air-landing Brigade.

The reconnaissance squadron, commanded by Major Freddie Gough, was under the orders of the 1st Parachute Brigade. This formation had been detailed to capture Arnhem Bridge and hold the close approaches to it. Brigadier Lathbury was conscious of the need for speed of movement and he had instructed Gough to hasten with the majority of his armed jeeps to the bridge as soon as they were unloaded from the gliders. Thereafter, the 2nd Battalion of The Parachute Regiment, travelling necessarily on foot, would relieve them and develop defences at either end of the bridge. The 3rd Battalion was to follow the 2nd, but on a parallel road to the north, immediately ready as a reinforcement in case of mishap while the 1st, in reserve, should prepare to occupy the high ground just north of Arnhem if they were not required for any unanticipated task. As most of the commanders had expected, however, there was much that it had not been possible to anticipate.

Their greeting on arrival went far beyond what they might have foreseen. Though they had known that the Dutch would welcome them, some men were hardly out of their parachute harness before whole families were upon them shaking their hands, patting their backs, sometimes kissing the newcomers, the liberators of their land. The national Dutch colour, orange, was appearing on dresses and jackets. The orange calendula was picked for the British to wear.

A sergeant of the 2nd Battalion, who had fought through the North African campaign and been wounded in the assault into Sicily described the situation this way: 'They just wouldn't let you go. I started calling out to the men in my platoon to get over to the rendezvous and slung on my webbing [equipment]. But the Dutch wanted to carry everything for us; they'd got their hands on packs, weapons – everything. My company commander asked a Dutchman if there were any Jerries about. "No," he said. "They've all run away now you've come to free us." I thought this was funny but every time we asked they said "They've all run away".' Clearly, some had not. Prisoners had already been taken on the edge of the dropping zone but they were the frightened occupants of a supply post. Others in Tettau's screen force had given themselves up. It took the 1st Parachute Brigade about forty minutes longer than they had planned to complete the rallying of their numbers, some of whom had been delayed by patients and nurses from the mental home nearby which was in use as a general hospital. It was getting on for 1530 hours when Lieutenant-Colonel John Frost, commanding the 2nd Battalion, set off along the road close to the Rhine bank for Arnhem and the bridge.

The reconnaissance squadron should, by this time, have been on its way. But it had not even assembled. 'I went by glider with A Troop vehicles,' said Lieutenant John Stevenson. 'We got down about 10 minutes before the [squadron] parachute party. It took us four and a half hours to unload and when I looked round for the remainder of the troop vehicles I found that, besides the jeep from our glider, only two others had got down so far.' As other members of the squadron searched, it became apparent that by an unhappy coincidence, the gliders which had failed to arrive were largely theirs. Brigadier Lathbury had now to rely on his infantry and instructed Frost to send men forward on his few jeeps.

The 3rd Battalion under Lieutenant-Colonel Fitch were now moving to the bridge by their own route. They, too, were delayed by the laughing, hand-clapping Dutch. 'You didn't like to be rude,' the Regimental Sergeant-Major commented, 'but some of our men just had to drop the apples and tomatoes and bits of bread that the people were

Above: CG4A glider unloading on US landing zone. *Below:* A CG4A crashes on landing

Above: Leaving the dropping zone. *Below:* Liberators perform the resupply mission

giving them. They were getting heaped up.' Parties were beckoned urgently to follow their new Dutch friends whom they asked for news of Germans. But instead of the enemy, they would find in some back garden or cottage a tray of drinks, a box of orange flowers, more apples, even cakes. There was a dreamlike quality to this sunny Sunday afternoon. Everything seemed so peaceful.

Yet many of the airborne soldiers were uneasy. In the distance, occasionally, there was the sound of rifle and machine gun fire. Suddenly they were in streets where there were no civilians to be seen and the windows were shuttered, the streets quiet. But if there was an enemy, the 3rd Battalion were asking themselves, who were they and where were they?

Much the same question was in the mind of General von Tettau, downstream at Rhenen, promoted now from controlling General Christiansen's screen on the Rhine to command the 'division' of local units. An addition to his many anxieties was the knowledge that the SS training units tended to refer to their local SS chiefs, who referred to his headquarters as 'the old men's club', to his chief of staff as 'the actor Ulrich'. Both Tettau and Ulrich had seen the air transport stream but neither knew exactly where the drop had taken place. Reports made during the afternoon by telephone were contradictory. Then, just after 1530 hours, a radio message was received from Sepp Krafft: 'Battalion Krafft is defending 2½ kilometres west of former position. Strong reconnaissance operation in progress. Night attack intended. Not been in action yet. One prisoner. Wolfheze occupied. Enemy reconnaissance observed in direction Wagenigen.'

Krafft was making the mistake of thinking his divisional commander knew what was happening. He was therefore astonished to receive this reply: '1620 hours. Enemy air landings at Driel, Culemborg, Zaltbommel and Nijmegen. Attack independently.'

Nijmegen apart, these points were miles from the DZs and LZs used. Krafft was perplexed. Wildly keen to show what his youthful SS soldiers could do, he was already issuing such orders as 'the enemy will be attacked continuously with shock troops' when he had less than 450 men of all ranks. Three detachments he sent out were either destroyed or forced away from their base as Lieutenant-Colonel Dobies' 1st Battalion moved towards Wolfheze. He was therefore delighted to see General Kussin, commander of Arnhem garrison, just after five pm, come to discover the situation for himself. After they had talked and Kussin had approved what he was doing, the general returned to his car but declined Krafft's advice to return by the Johanna Hoeve road north of the railway.

'I have no time to spare', said the general, more correct than he knew. For when he took the road to Oosterbeek, he and his companions ran into an ambush of the 3rd Battalion and they were all killed by a burst from a light machine gun.

Though Krafft thought he had been holding off the enemy, he had largely been fighting shadows. But now Harzer's advanced elements were appearing to give substance to resistance.

Probably the first person to recognise the danger was Major Freddie Gough. With the few vehicles available to his reconnaissance squadron, he had discovered that both the 2nd and 3rd Battalions were opposed on their routes into Arnhem. He therefore tried to bypass these by looping northward but soon found himself under ranging fire of several high velocity heavy weapons. Field glasses showed that these were mounted on armoured vehicles. Returning through Wolfheze, he warned Dobie's battalion. On the Johanna Hoeve road, the battalion advanced until they were quickly engaged by four or five machine guns sited in an arc round the first cross roads. It was Krafft's right hand company, which was evicted by a quick assault. What concerned Dobie was the sight of several tanks in rear. His 6-pounder troop drove them off but he wisely forbore to follow directly with his infantry, preferring to switch to the Ede road to the north. As they began to move, five tanks and fifteen Panzer Grenadier half tracks appeared from the east. Any move by the parachute battalion further to the

'I have no time to spare . . . ' General Kussin's car ambushed

north must be cut off by the enemy in their tracked transport. Dobie decided to skip back to the south, hoping to find a gap between the two roads – it was that or a withdrawal to Wolfheze under pressure.

They broke contact and sought cover among a number of little copses. One rifle company had lost more than half its number. The other two had twelve and seventeen casualties respectively. As all this had occurred between 1600 and 2000 hours, with no tactical advantage gained, the situation was becoming critical. Unable to make contact on his radio with brigade headquarters or any other unit, Dobie decided that he must nonetheless find his way to the high ground as originally ordered.

None of the main divisional wireless communications were working satisfactorily. Amongst the pine plantations and towns of Holland the sets had failed, somewhat as the divisional signals commander had feared. He had been begging the War Office to provide a more compact and powerful set for airborne forces and he had failed to persuade some of his colleagues in the division to release more seats and freight in aircraft for additional signal stations.

Unable to talk by voice or key to any of his commanders, General Urquhart took the practical view that he must seek them out himself. He left his small headquarters at the edge of the landing areas to set off by jeep with a signaller. Soon he came on Frost's battalion headquarters close to the Rhine bank. After brushing aside Krafft's local defences, the battalion had pushed on but were now halted while the leading company dealt with an armoured car supported by infantry. Frost was somewhere ahead. Leaving a message urging speed, Urquhart returned along the road looking for Lathbury.

Lathbury's anxiety for speed of advance – and the fact that his radio had little contact – had drawn him to follow first Frost and now Fitch. The 3rd Battalion had run into Krafft's left hand company which gave them a demonstration of brave if often unskilled fighting. It was this battle into which General Kussin ran at about 1730 hours and was killed. At 1800 hours, leaving their dead and six prisoners, the SS youngsters withdrew to the north. A company of the 3rd Battalion had yet to move off when mortar bombs began to fall, whether from Krafft's base plates or Harzer's we do not know. But Urquhart arrived to find Lathbury in the middle of this bombardment and soon the general's jeep was hit, his signaller wounded. A mile beyond, Fitch's foremost troops had also been halted by more of Harzer's battle group. It was coming on towards darkness. Urquhart had been fired on several times on his journey from Frost's to Fitch's battalion. Close by, the bodies of General Kussin and his party provided an object lesson. It is not surprising that he decided to spend the night with Lathbury and the 3rd Battalion.

From the road near the river bank, there was further heavy firing and an immense explosion. Frost's battalion was continuing to force its way forward and after nightfall the radio in Brigadier Lathbury's jeep announced that they were on the bridge.

West of Wolfheze, Brigadier Pip Hicks with one and a half battalions of the air-landing brigade waited in position round DZ 'Y' for Monday morning when 4th Parachute Brigade should descend to join the battle. They dealt briskly with the attempts of Tettau's division to penetrate their ranks. Between their posts and the Rhine, the light batteries were in action.

South of Arnhem, south of the Rhine, the 82nd and 101st had been experiencing their own series of perilous adventures.

The aircraft carrying the 82nd appeared punctually to discover the letter O laid out in yellow panels with a nearby exposure of violet smoke to mark their dropping and landing zones. Amongst the 7,227 men jumping was E Company of 504th Parachute Infantry, a company with the special mission of seizing the south end of the Maas bridge at Grave.

As the C-47s swept over the final mile of their outward journey, Lieutenant John Thompson was standing in the doorway of one of them, waiting for the signal to lead fifteen men of E Company in their jump. He noticed that, as the green light flashed the signal to go they were passing over buildings. Wisely he paused a few seconds to 'jump on a field just southwest of Grave bridge.' Recovering, they saw they were only 700 yards from their target.

'... spasmodic firing could be heard from the town,' he reported. '... two men landed in a drainage ditch and had a hard time getting out. Radio contact with the company was immediately tried but we could not get through. Seeing that we were very close to the bridge and knowing that this was our primary mission, I sent a messenger back to where the company was assembling and told the company commander that we were proceeding towards the bridge. We worked our way down various canals wading in water up to our necks. By this time firing from the town and the buildings around us had increased considerably and there was now firing coming from a camouflaged flak tower on the southern approach to the bridge. As we neared [it] we could see German soldiers running to and from a power plant which was about 50 yards due west of the bridge. They made several trips carrying something in their arms. We waited until they made about three trips and then raked the area with machine gun fire. Later, when we overran the power plant we found four dead German soldiers and one wounded. They had apparently been carrying their equipment and blankets. As we got closer, we were surprised to see two trucks coming down the highway from Grave towards the bridge. My leading scout fired, killing the driver. The truck careered off the road with the German soldiers scrambling to get out. The second truck stopped and the soldiers in it jumped out and deployed... We continued to work our way along in defilade towards the flak tower and the bridge. The flak tower continued to fire but by now the fire was going over our heads. My bazooka man worked his way forward and fired three rounds, two of them going into the top of the tower. The gun then ceased firing. In it we found two Ger-

Americans move through village on way to Hell's Highway

mans dead and one wounded. We took over the gun and engaged the guns on the far side. All communication wires leading across the bridge were cut and a roadblock was set up at the southern end. About this time we were surprised to see two automobiles tearing down the highway towards the bridge from Grave. They were destroyed when they got close... Shortly after this, a patrol came from my battalion across the bridge...'

Although the enemy overcome here belonged to the inferior Korps Feldt, this timely and determined action by fourteen enlisted men under Lieutenant Thompson snatched intact the bridge over the Maas, despite strong defences and a complete system of demolitions. They might have been tempted to wait for the remainder of E Company but fortunately they did not; for the rest of the company had been landed too close to the edge of Grave, from which a hot fire fell among them. Unable to move round it in daylight, the company commander established a roadblock against enemy transport coming up from the south.

North of the Maas, Colonel Reuben Tucker, commander of the 504th, had also to capture a bridge across the Maas-Waal canal. The rifle company sent to Malden had begun to charge the defences when it was blown up. At Heumen, a company under Captain Thomas Helgeson was kept from the southern end by machine gun fire, several weapons being sighted in a concrete pillbox on an island. To charge on was out of the question but one squad crawled forward to set up a machine gun on the bank and while this was fired, the company second-in-command dashed across the bridge with another officer, a corporal and a radio operator. Another officer and six men found a boat which they used to cross the water at a distance. Captain Helgeson feared that the Germans, so plainly surrounded, must now fire the demolitions but the afternoon waned as the fire fight continued intermittently. At dusk, a specialist squad from headquarters company slipped through the deepening shadows to the opposite side of the bridge

Colonel Shields Warren, Jr (taken post-war)

Colonel Harry W O Kinnard, Jr (taken post-war)

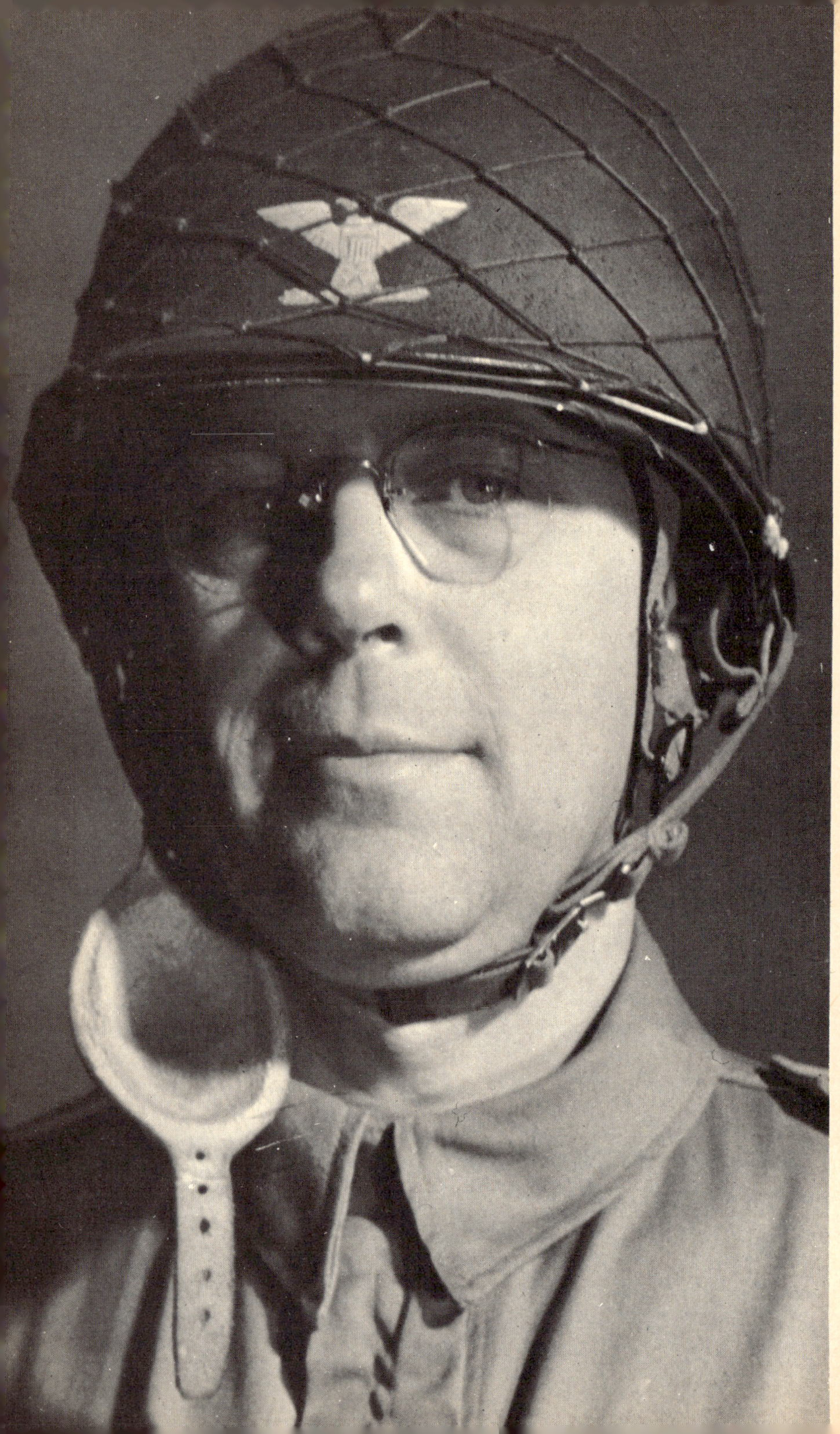

structure to find and cut the demolition circuits. With darkness the island was stormed and the crossing captured.

General Gavin had now secured two of the three essential crossings. But he was unhappily aware that the bridge at Nijmegen had still to be taken. One of his regiments, the 505th, had necessarily been committed to the capture of the high ground round Groesbeek and the first shallow reconnaissance of the Reichswald forest to the west, in which it had been feared that there might be armour. But the heights were too extensive for one regiment; and thus Colonel Roy E Lindquist's 508th Parachute Infantry were obliged to take the northerly sector in addition to the tasks of clearing and holding the landing zone for the gliders arriving on the 18th and, most important of all, capturing the Nijmegen bridge.

In the performance of these tasks there had arisen a misunderstanding. General Gavin was clear in his own mind that at his briefing in England he had ordered Lindquist to send a battalion (that of Lieutenant-Colonel Shields Warren Jr) to capture the Waal bridge 'without delay after landing'. Lindquist believed that he was not to send a battalion off until he had a battalion on the high ground and the prospective LZ secured. It was evening when General Gavin discovered the omission. He told Lindquist 'to delay not a second longer and get the bridge as quickly as possible with Warren's battalion'. Fortunately, Warren had already reached the south-eastern outskirts of Nijmegen where he had established a defence and sent into the town at about 1830 hours a patrol – one rifle platoon from C Company and his intelligence section. They had just departed when Warren was told to capture the bridge at once.

In haste, Warren sent messages to A and B Companies to meet him at a rendezvous on the edge of the town at 1900 hours, when he would lead them forward with a Dutch guide. At 1900 hours, he met A Company but there was no sign of B and no news from the patrol of C Company. At 2000 hours he assumed correctly that B Company was lost and the small headquarters

Left: Colonel Roy E Lindquist. *Above:* Allied dead

party, accompanied by the guide, set off with A Company and a detachment of heavy weapons.

There were no civilians in the shadowed streets. All was silent. At first they moved with caution, searching buildings until, finding nothing, Colonel Warren sensibly decided to risk a chance encounter. He directed the column along the dark corridor of the Groesbeekschweg, a main road running towards the centre of Nijmegen. Moving silently on the rubber soles of their jumping boots, the paratroopers reached the circular park of the Keizer Karel Plein, an area from which a boulevard stretched directly to the bridge. The scouts began to spread out until a burst of fire was opened on the column from the park ahead.

It was now 2200 hours. The company commander shook out his platoons, while his mortar crews set up their weapons. As they were reorganising with urgent whispers, a traffic column was heard to enter a side street nearby. With much shouting and the clash of studded boots on the paving, men were heard alighting.

What they were listening to was the arrival of the leading battle group of the 10th SS Panzer Division. The feeble units of Korps Feldt had been reinforced in the nick of time. Occupying Nijmegen bridge defences was a company of Panzer Grenadiers.

Elsewhere, there was better news for Gavin. The company sent to the Reichswald Forest had found no trace of German armour. At Grave, E Company commander had entered the town shortly after darkness to discover the basis for an extraordinary noise. He found the town deserted by the enemy and the Dutch celebrating by singing a local version of an old British army marching song, 'A long way to Tipperary'.

Shortly after the opening of General Taylor's divisional radio net, it was discovered that one battalion – from 501st Parachute Infantry – had been dropped three miles to the north-west of its dropping zone; otherwise, all 6,769 parachutists had come down within the divisional boundary. The commander of the displaced unit was Lieutenant-Colonel Harry W O Kinnard Jr, who shed a small detachment to collect and guard the equipment bundles while the remainder marched at a smart pace to their destinations. They took an undefended bridge across the narrow Aa river and suppressed abruptly the half-hearted resistance offered by the detachment of Korps Feldt in Veghel town. Here, shortly, they welcomed another American battalion entering from the south. By 1630 hours, Colonel Howard R Johnson of the 501st reported that his regiment was in possession of the Aa road bridge, Veghel, the bridge across the Zuid Willems canal, and a strong road block from Eerde village to the main road running south to St Oedenrode.

Lieutenant - Colonel Patrick Cassidy's battalion of the 502nd had been dropped in another regiment's zone but this he turned to good account by capturing the little garrison in St Oedenrode and a second road bridge across the winding Dommel stream.

Further south, the 506th Parachute Infantry had pushed down towards the village of Zon, hastening to capture the road bridge across the Wilhelmina canal. Leading the column was Major James L La Prade's battalion which, hoping to gain time and surprise, passed round to the west of the village. About a mile from the canal, they came under the fire of a single 88mm gun dug into the edge of the Zonsche forest with a small infantry screen nearby. On their left flank, the fire from this post prevented them from moving across the open ground directly ahead. La Prade had either to attack it or move right, into the village. He chose to attack but sixty precious minutes had passed before the Germans were overcome.

The other two battalions of the regiment, believing that they had only to clear Zon itself, had an experience similar to that of 1st Parachute Brigade at Arnhem. Though there were few Germans to be cleared out, the obstacle to progress was the mob of cheering Dutch citizens who rushed to greet the soldiers between scattered shooting. This part of the 506th was emerging from Zon on the south side just as La Prade, having resumed his

Warm welcome

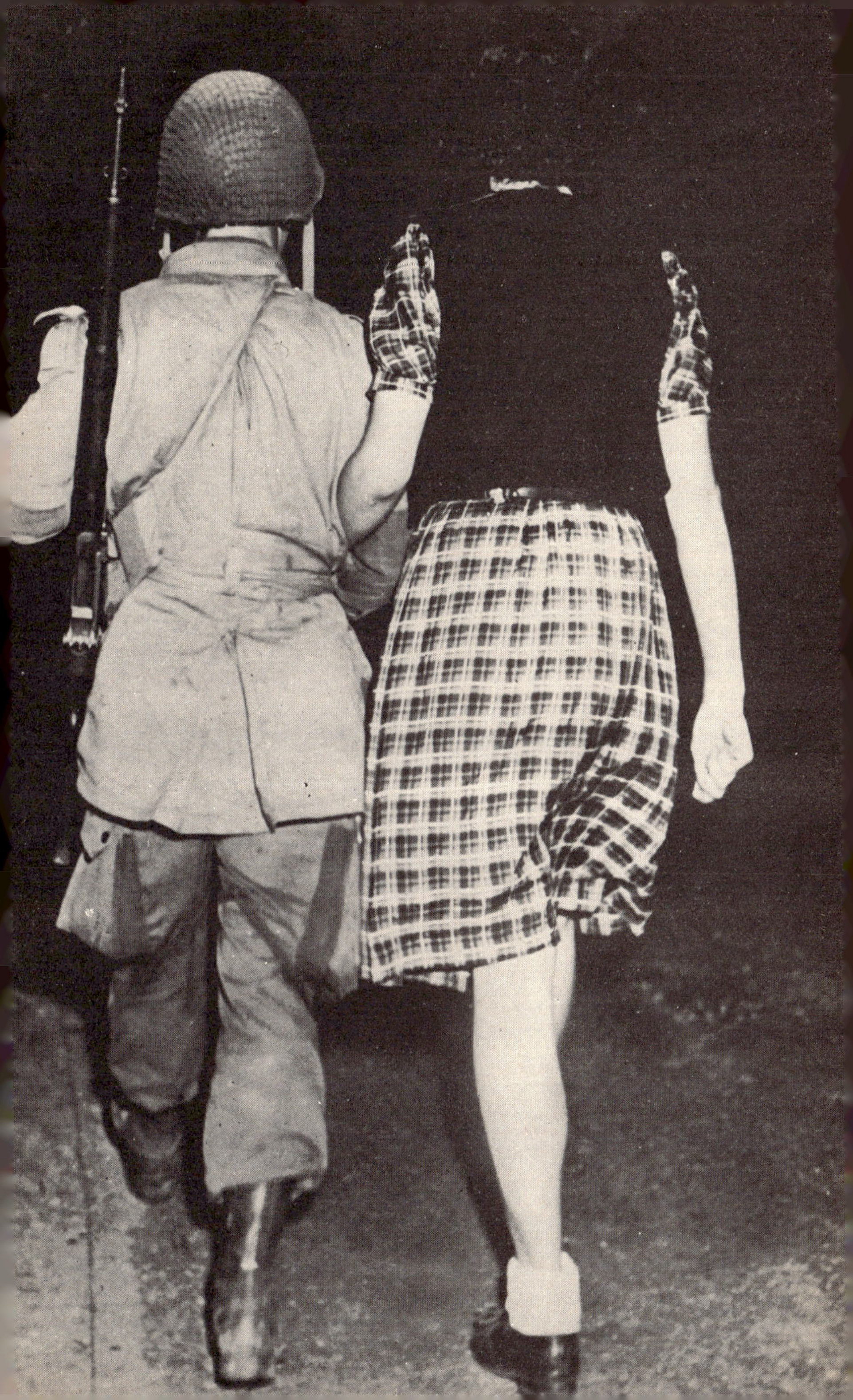

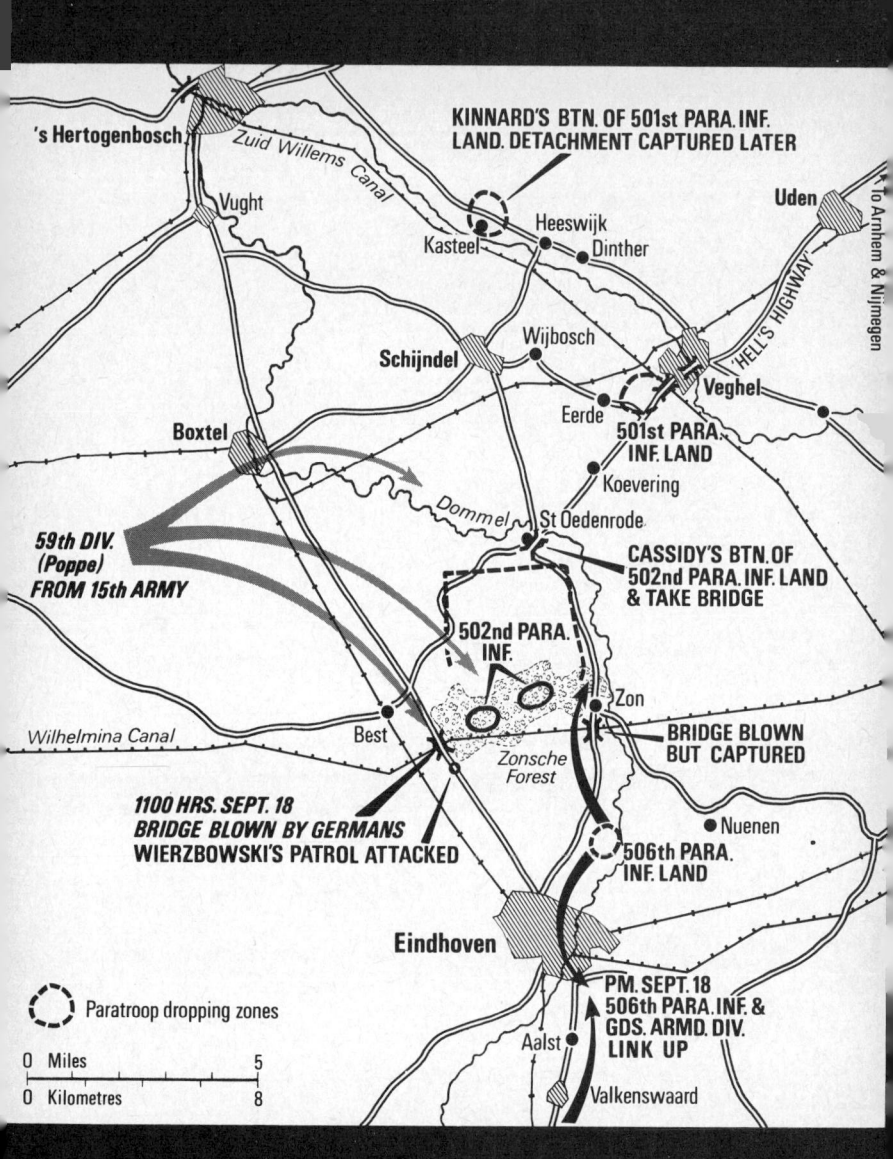

The situation in the 101st Airborne Division's area on 18th September

Second wave at Grave

march, appeared from the west. All three battalions were in sight of the road bridge when the boom and flash of exploding charges told their own story. Running to the bank, La Prade dived into the water and swam across, followed by several of his acutely disappointed command. A small boat was found in a shed and this was borrowed to ferry over more men. The gallant battalion commander, dripping with water and chilled as clouds began to obscure the evening sun, drove out the Germans on the south bank while a platoon of engineers began to improvise a footbridge for the remainder of the regiment.

The loss of the bridge was vexing but not irrecoverable. What concerned General Taylor more as the night developed were signs of increasing pressure from the west. His division was charged with opening the main road from Eindhoven towards the 82nd at Grave – the road he had named 'Hell's Highway'. It was almost forty miles long, indefensible, in fact, even when his whole division was down, against any determined thrust by the enemy at any one point. He did not know whether the main German attack would be developed from the east or the west; they might even use a simultaneous thrust from both directions. Half in fun but otherwise in common sense, he intended to treat the problem in the way that early Americans had dealt with maintaining an open railroad in the Indian wars: with secure bases from which he could mount sorties against raiders.

The first straws in the wind were seen at Kasteel, where Harry Kinnard had left his injured men with the party collecting bundles. When Kinnard sent back to find these men they had disappeared but, ominously, there were bloodstained bandages by the château. Forty-eight American paratroopers would not have been captured by a roaming band from Korps Feldt unless it was a very large one. The probability was that better troops were arriving. The second disturbing item of news was from Colonel Michaelis' 502nd. A strong patrol with engineers had been sent to capture and dismantle the demolitions on the road bridge at Best on the western side of the Zonsche forest. Though not directly on Hell's Highway, its possession would afford, as a useful bonus, a second bridge across the Wilhelmina canal. Michaelis reported that he had sent after this a company which was under heavy attack and he had despatched the remainder of the battalion to that flank. On landing, the Dutch had assured Taylor that there was only a tiny German detachment at Best. Where had this stronger and apparently determined body come from? Who had captured Harry Kinnard's men at Kasteel?

With nightfall came a cold driving rain. With darkness the apprehensions of the day were, everywhere, from Arnhem to Zon, heightened and exacerbated. At Arnhem, Urquhart had no contact with anyone other than Lathbury and the 3rd Battalion of The Parachute Regiment. Neither Gavin nor Taylor could speak to Arnhem. Browning was unable to raise XXX Corps. Yet despite their discomforts and apprehensions, wherever they could do so within their perimeters and sentry posts, men slept soundly after the many fatigues of the long day.

Garden opens

'At 11 a.m. on Sunday morning, 17th September, 1944' we are told by Lieutenant-General Sir Brian Horrocks, 'I climbed up an iron ladder leading to the flat roof of a large factory on the south bank of the Meuse-Escaut canal which was to be my command post for the opening stages of the battle. It was a peaceful, sunny Sunday morning . . . .

'Then I heard on the wireless that the airborne divisions were on their way. Suddenly the armada appeared overhead . . . . I ordered "Zero hour, 1435 hours". At 2 pm, precisely, there was a sudden deafening roar and a noise as though an express train was passing overhead. Our guns had opened their counter-artillery programme and the battle of Arnhem was on.'

Manhandling their heavy shells from stack to breech, the British, Belgian and Dutch gunners were kept hard at work. As the counter-bombardment programme switched from target to target, 144 field guns began a rolling barrage over the narrow frontage of the corridor. Thirty-six medium guns opened fire to thicken it.

Quite separately, 120 field guns and a battery of 8-inch heavy guns began to drop concentrations of shells on troop positions, headquarters and vehicle parks selected by ground observers and air reconnaissance during the preceding days. From zero hour, eight rocket-firing Typhoons swooped down on to German positions on either side of the road leading to Valkenswaard and Eindhoven – the southernmost stretch of Hell's Highway.

At zero hour, the commander of the leading tank troop, a lieutenant of the 2nd Irish Guards named Keith Heathcote, brought his handset to his mouth to say, 'Driver advance'. Squeaking and creaking on their tracks, the tanks began to lumber forward towards the smoke of their own shellfire, across the Dutch frontier.

The leading squadron was perhaps 1,000 yards from its start point when the boom and clangour of anti-tank action began in their rear. Very

Tanks of the Guards Armoured Division on the way to Eindhoven

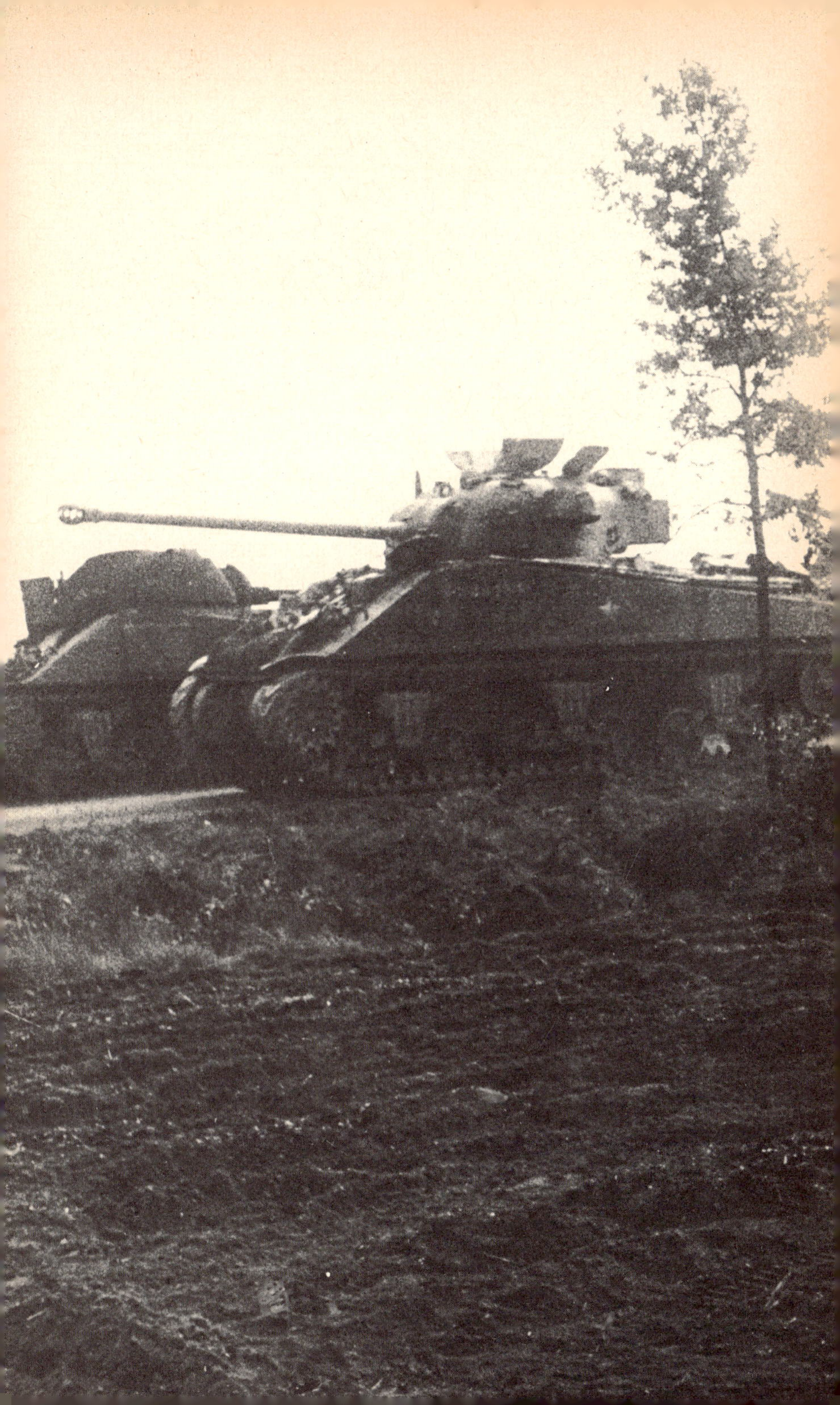

A column of transport vehicles passing along a Dutch road as the 11th Armoured Division advance

quickly, nine of the Irish Guards tanks were knocked out. As soon as their anti-tank guns opened fire, German infantry concealed in trenches fired their *panzerfaust* launchers at the tanks, their MG 34s at the infantry riding with the second squadron. In retaliation, the tanks' machine guns were turned on every hedgerow and woodland but the enemy they were fighting were old hands at battle ambush: both towed 88mm and self-propelled guns were dug in under camouflage; the infantry trenches were cut into banks from which their fire crossed in enfilade.

The anti-tank network and the infantry protecting it from bullet or bayonet assault had been designed by a parachutist colonel named Walther. In his *Kampfgruppe* behind the canal were two battalions from 6th Parachute Regiment, two from the 9th and 10th SS Infantry Divisions – not to be confused with those at Arnhem – and a unit of German criminals, the 6th Penal Battalion. The main road divided parachutists and SS conveniently. Observing that their first elementary ripostes had failed to suppress the accurate and deliberate German fire, the Guards revealed that they were also far from being novices. Tanks and infantry co-operated in a series of small actions while Typhoons, called from a 'cab-rank' overhead, struck at strongpoints with dazzling accuracy on the very edge of the battle. Slowly, these measures forced open the corridor.

At 1700 hours, concerned to hasten the pace of the advance, the Guards prepared a concerted push. More Typhoons of 83 Group mustered in waves. The medium guns repeated their rolling barrage and grudgingly the enemy gave way, withdrawing to a greater distance. The advanced guard of XXX Corps accelerated along the highway while from the rear two battalions of the line started their search for the many pockets of Walther's men unable to get out and unwilling to surrender.

The commander of the Guards Armoured Division, Major-General

Allan Adair, had been ordered to reach Valkenswaard by the evening of D-day; and this the Guards had accomplished, an advance of six miles. Though Horrocks had hoped that they might be in Eindhoven at nightfall, it had become clear that, on such a narrow front and against an enemy of high calibre, it was not feasible. The Irish Guards battle group deserved their rest as they settled down after replenishment of vehicles and a hot meal. Nearby, the Welsh Guards group, warned to continue on the 18th, had no illusions that *Kampfgruppe* Walther had conceded them a free passage to Eindhoven.

Indeed, there was an expectation throughout the whole of XXX Corps that the enemy would continue a stubborn resistance next day. This being so, it was surely a mistake to leave the initiatives of the night to the Germans. Concealed by the darkness, Oberst Walther was able to revise and reinforce his defences along the road to Eindhoven. A number of Panthers, the Pzkw. V tank, were deployed to replace the anti-tank guns knocked out during the 17th. Two minor and uncertain contacts apart, the reinforcing German infantry were able to dig their trenches freely.

To the south, XXX Corps used the night to complete internal preparations for fighting next day and for rest. Infantry patrolling was limited and scarcely productive: no attempt was made to raid extensively into *Kampfgruppe* Walther to inhibit its redeployment by alarm and confusion. The Germans were wont to say on Bradley's front, 'We'll begin movement at midnight when the Americans will stop'. On the route to Arnhem, it stopped for the majority of the British column, many of whom had not seen a minute of action on the 17th, by 2200 hours.

Right and left of XXX Corps, VIII and XII Corps displayed a similar lack of enterprise.

The first reports of Market Garden to reach Hitler's headquarters were made by the Luftwaffe air observation and warning branch. A little later they received the account of Field-Marshal Model's escape from Oosterbeek, faithfully relayed by General Kussin. The Führer reacted with the intermittent

A King Tiger knocked out in the corridor

displays of emotional excitement characteristic of him.

Recently he had come to recognise the menace of the western Allies' advance; now he perceived a mortal danger. He railed at the Luftwaffe for permitting such an operation as Market, calling them traitors for the way in which they repeatedly failed him. Speaking of Model's adventure, he reminded the Nazi hierarchy that they were not immune from such an operation. 'At any rate', he said, 'the business is so dangerous that you must understand clearly, if such a mess happens here – here I sit with my whole supreme command – . . . Well, then, this is the most worthwhile catch, that's obvious. I would not hesitate to risk two parachute divisions here if with one blow I could get my hands on the whole German command.'

They did not realise – nor did Model – that the Allies were unaware that they were landing parachutists next to Headquarters, Army Group B. This misapprehension helped to sustain a general parachute scare which continued for some days. On 18th September, Runstedt's headquarters went so far as to pass down to Army Group B a story that the allies had landed an American airborne division in Warsaw.

More practically, the Führer and his staff had to decide what could be done to counter the airborne assault and the ground operation which it clearly presaged. They were still without a fresh division, organised and ready in the central reserve. Runstedt was transferring the 107th Panzer Brigade from Aachen and the 280th Assault Gun Brigade to join Student's army. Poppe's 59th Division had already passed across into the fighting from Fifteenth Army and Zangen had nothing else available. Possibly smarting from Hitler's abuse, Göring was able to offer the last of his parachute force under General Meindl at Cologne, the newest and the least trained men. The jet fighter-bombers were also ready to operate. Two squadrons of the Me 262s were now able to take off from the Rheine area to airfields nearer the Netherlands. A promise was given that they would fly on the 18th against the Allies.

107

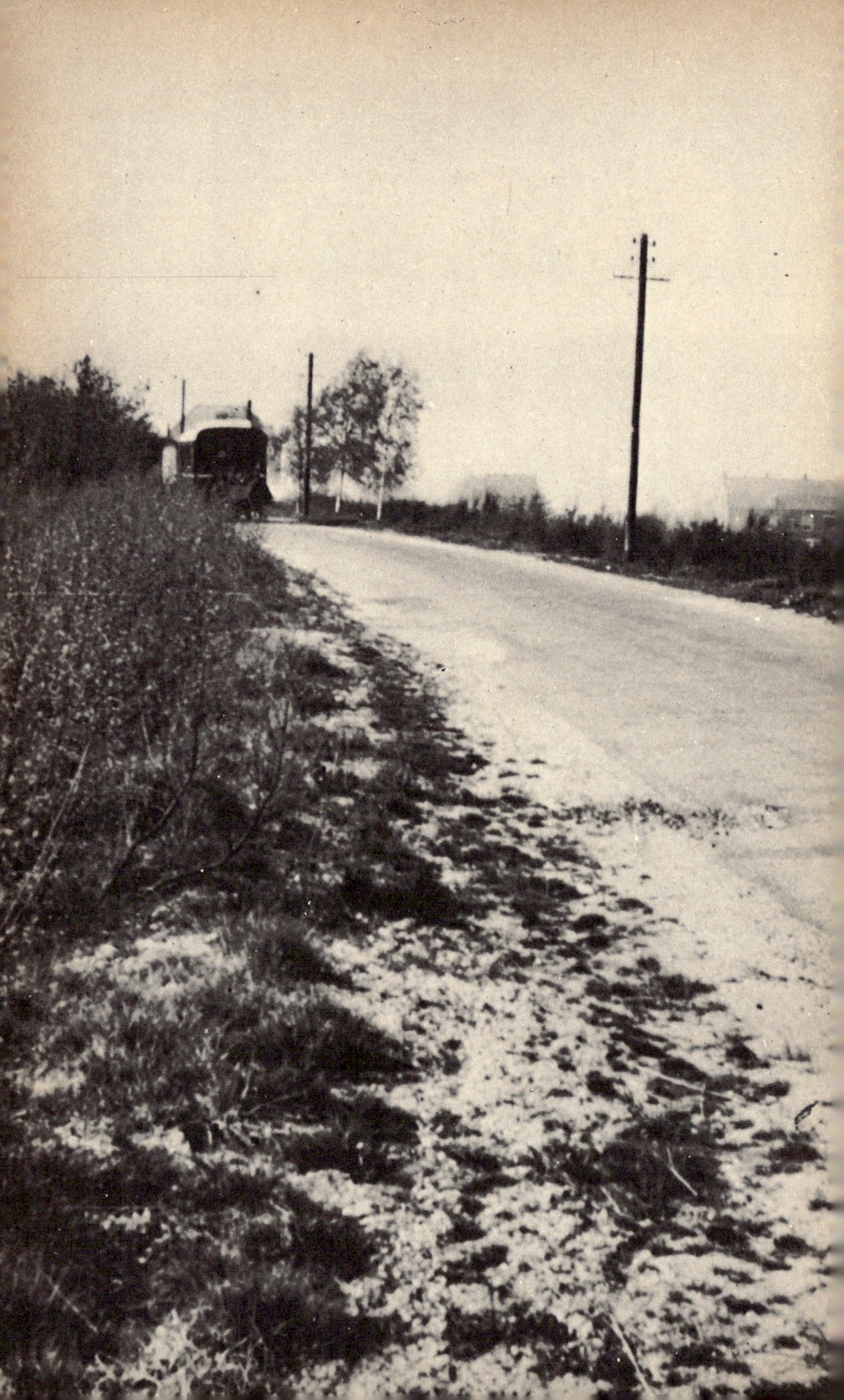

Left: Hell's Highway, Venlo – Grave.
Above: Major-General Allan Adair, commander of the Guards' Armoured Division

Monday, 18th September

A considerate commander, General Horrocks made it a practice to issue orders as early as possible each evening so as to permit those required to fight next day the maximum amount of rest. He had an articulate and practical staff. The orders given to the corps for 18th September ensured that additional infantry would be available to support the Guards in the close country ahead and endorsed the need to press the advance towards Arnhem. When the weather report was read, the chief gunner recognised that he must be ready to provide for all the supporting fire next day; it was said that the evening rain clouds would persist and restrict, probably prevent air operations for the next twenty-four hours.

At 0600 hours on Monday morning, the Welsh Guards group began their encounter with *Kampfgruppe* Walther. Once more, the 2nd Household Cavalry reconnoitred and probed the countryside ahead. By 1230 hours, two of their armoured cars had sneaked into Eindhoven while the main force was battling through the woods south of Aalst. In Eindhoven, they found Colonel Sink and the 506th Parachute Infantry, heroes of the city, struggling to free themselves from the welcoming burghers in order to capture what remained of the German garrison.

Colonel Sink's regiment had passed over the Wilhelmina canal at Zon by midnight using the footbridge prepared by their parachute engineers. With very limited resources, this had been strengthened to accept a few light vehicles but it was incapable of bearing trucks, still less tanks. General Taylor was therefore more than ever determined to capture the bridge at Best. Early in the morning, Colonel Michaelis sent a second battalion of the 502nd to join the fighting on the edge of the Zonsche forest. Equally, the majority of General Poppe's 59th Division were concentrating to force the Americans back. Being infinitely stronger and backed by artillery, they came close to overpowering the advancing battalions until a brief period of finer weather permitted an air strike by a

German troops move in toward the British dropping zone

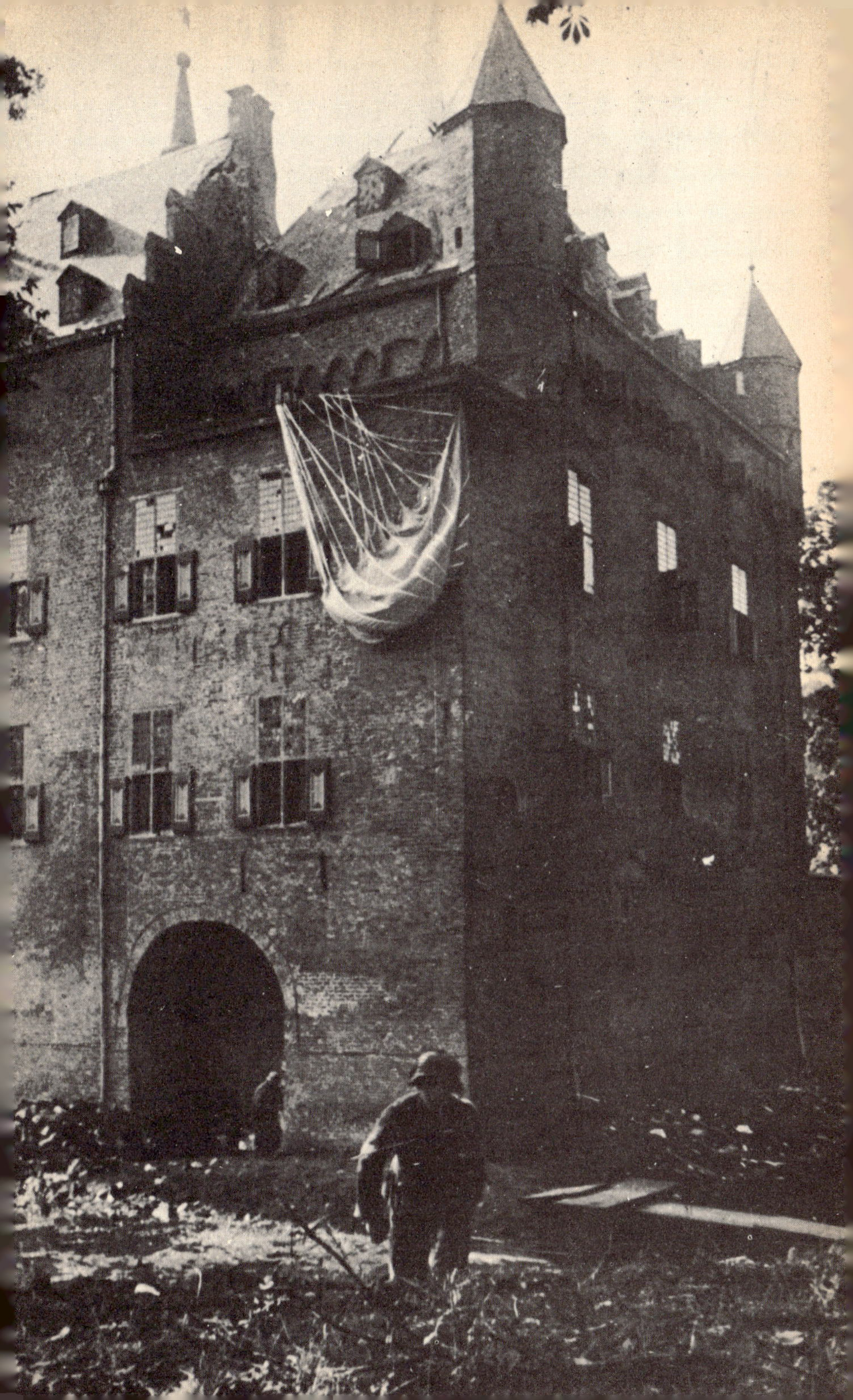

flight of P-47s. The two battalions drew back to combine their defences. In the fighting, one of the commanding officers was killed.

Close to the steel and concrete road bridge lay the patrol sent out during the previous afternoon from the 502nd. Its commander was Lieutenant Wierzbowski. He had been despatched with over eighty infantry and engineers but on the night march, during several encounters with the enemy, mistakes, panic and casualties had reduced the party. He now mustered fifteen beside himself. After dawn on the 18th, they heard firing and over a period of hours the rattle and bang grew closer. What they could hear was the approach of first one and then the other battalion from their regiment – but so could the German engineers on the bridge. At 1100 hours, fearing capture, they shattered the concrete and steel in a single loud explosion. Then the battle noises faded again. From the bridge, a German platoon came to attack Wierzbowski's patrol, killing one and wounding four of the survivors. They were driven off. In the afternoon, the two armoured cars of the British Household Cavalry which had reached Eindhoven came into view on the far side of the canal and for a time their machine guns helped to rebuff the persistent German attempts to destroy this determined little post. Between actions, for the remainder of the afternoon, both British and American radios on the canal tried to discover what was happening in the 101st's area.

If they had been successful, they would have discovered that it was an afternoon of inactivity. The battalions in the Zonsche forest were baulked of their wish to capture the Best bridge but denied equally the attempts of the 59th Division to overwhelm them. The third battalion of the regiment, Lieutenant - Colonel Patrick Cassidy's at Odenroode, made good use of his time to improve the defences. There was every sign that they were shortly to be assailed. At Veghel, the 501st were subject to the same reconnaissance and probing. General Taylor was relieved to see two glider battalions arrive that afternoon, delayed by the weather, with more vehicles and radios, supplies and a pair of bulldozers. He greatly regretted however, the absence of his artillery.

To the north, the immediate problem occupying General Gavin was the capture of the Nijmegen bridge. After their night encounter in the centre of Nijmegen, the 10th SS battle group had counterattacked the company of the 508th until, ending a confused struggle in the darkness, both sides had drawn apart. To the relief of Colonel Warren, his B Company, drawn by the sound of firing, suddenly reported and he at once asked his regimental commander to release C Company in order that he might attack the bridge in strength. While the conversation took place over the radio, a Dutch civilian approached Captain Jonathan Adams, commanding A Company, to say that the mechanism for the demolition of the road bridge was housed in the post office, a few blocks to the north. He offered to guide him there. With his battalion commander's permission, Captain Adams took a patrol away with the Dutchman who skilfully guided them through numerous side streets to the edge of their destination. After receiving a simple plan of action whispered in the darkness, the paratroops stormed the building and overwhelmed the German guards. The demolition mechanism was quickly destroyed. But when they came to leave the building it was surrounded by German troops. Captain Adams had to revise quickly his ideas and block the entrances. He was evidently faced with a siege.

Meanwhile, Colonel Warren had made some headway with his attack on the bridge, advancing close to the southern end. Whatever his hopes, the fire from the immediate area of the crossing, a weak German attack on his own position and the light of dawn kept him from capturing it. Captain Adams and his patrol had not returned, and C Company was still in regimental reserve. A renewed attack must therefore depend upon B Company and a part of A. Shortly, General Gavin arrived to find the battalion headquarters at work in the Marienboom School.

It did not take the shrewd Gavin long to see that, scattered and tired after eighteen hours continuous activity, Warren's force needed to be concentrated and given a rest. Ordering them to draw back, the divisional commander was at the same time concerned to try again to capture the bridge which, so close now, was still far from being in his possession.

There was little to spare from the essential defences; the 504th were holding the Maas crossing at Grave and the Maas-Waal canal; the 505th was defending the greater part of the heights and the southern glider zone but could not also embrace the northern sector of the ridge; thus the 508th had to commit part of its strength north of Groesbeek, part in Nijmegen. The northern glider sector would also need to be cleared by midday for the follow-up landings.

In such circumstances, General Gavin decided to send a single company to try to capture the bridge supported by the fire of his parachute artillery and all the mortars within range. He believed that, approaching from a new direction – the south – a small determined body might still carry off the task with surprise. It may also be that he was half-inclined to believe that the Germans were withdrawing from the city. During the night, a railway train had passed through the centre of the divisional area without check, though all the passengers aboard were enemy soldiers. Until it passed, no one thought to stop it. Observing this success, a German commander had filled a second train at Nijmegen station. But aroused and ready, the 82nd had contrived an efficient block across the tracks down the line, round which an ambush waited. The prisoners taken were fearful and irresolute, mostly from garrison and other staffs. They claimed that orders had been given to evacuate the city.

So G Company of the 508th Regiment marched down from its position on top of Hill 64 towards the Waal and the bridge. At 0745 hours that morning they passed a radio message to say that they were moving to an assault location. The Dutch crowds, wearing their orange favours, fell back and they were alone.

Approach through Oosterbeek

Above: 20mm flak gun is set up on the German barrier defence in Arnhem.
Below: German troops in positions outside the city

Above: British carrier knocked out on 17th September. *Below:* Harzer's panzers move in

US paratroops street fighting in Holland

What General Gavin did not know was that the reconnaissance battalion of the 9th, in addition to the group of the 10th SS Panzer Division, had now reached the Nijmegen area where they had taken local flak units under their control. The 20mm and 88mm guns of the latter were the first to fire on G Company, followed soon by machine guns, rifles and carbines as Captain Novak, their commander, led them in a dash along the sides of the street. Other German posts on the far side of the river opened fire. Rightly, the company was halted. They took up their own fire positions in the buildings at hand.

As the morning wore on, Germans were seen to be infiltrating westward from the Reichswald forest. An attack developed against the company defending the southern landing zone for the gliders. Continuous skirmishing vexed the paratroops until at last, with some artillery support, they made a sortie to clear the many groups infesting the area. They were found to be from the 406th (*Landesschützen*) Division of Korps Feldt. On the northern zone, about 500 Germans were in occupation with sixteen 20mm anti-aircraft guns which closed towards Beek. Novak's company was still in Nijmegen; there was no resistance to hand. Called from their rest at 1000 hours, Warren's battalion made a forced march from Nijmegen to rendezvous with their C Company shortly after midday. The gliders were due at 1300 hours. With so little time in hand, Lieutenant-Colonel Shields Warren Jr, spread his battalion out quickly and gave the simple order to charge. They emerged from cover and began to run downhill towards the Germans and their guns. The enemy infantry wavered, then ran, some into the fire of their own flak weapons which drove off to new positions out of sight. Warren's companies reached the far side of the landing zone just as the aircraft and gliders appeared. They had taken 150 prisoners and were to find another fifty bodies when they returned across the zone later. Now they stood back as the gliders flew in to a safe landing.

Gavin was more comfortable with the arrival of his remaining artillery, though he needed urgently the glider infantry. He felt instinctively that the Reichswald forest would soon disgorge something more menacing than detachments from Korps Feldt and he had still to capture Nijmegen bridge. He had learned, too, in the latter part of the morning that Arnhem was occupied by strong forces. His liaison officer with the Dutch resistance movement, Captain Brestebeurje, had been shown details of the private telephone system of the Gelderland Electricity Company, still fully operating. It was used to pass quick simple news items and one had come from the power station at Arnhem. It said: 'Germans beating back British.'

As Sunday evening passed, General Willi Bittrich grew restless. In the afternoon he had told Model what additional units he would need to destroy the British north of the Rhine; a bill of reinforcement set out in detailed terms as both men now knew from Student how much of the British airborne division had arrived and what they were planning to do. Later, he had heard from Harzer that his reconnaissance battalion was on its way to Nijmegen while the remainder of 9th SS Panzer Division, as *Kampfgruppe* Harzer, drew into Oosterbeek and Arnhem. One battle group of 10th SS Panzer had also departed for Nijmegen but after further thought he had kept back the majority in their divisional area, ready to move either into Arnhem or to reinforce Nijmegen.

Reports grew vaguer and fewer: nothing had been seen in Arnhem and there were no signs of the Americans in Nijmegen. Bittrich decided to go into Arnhem to see how matters stood in the city and he drove to the garrison headquarters. All but a small watch were manning defences and General Kussin was said to be visiting the SS Training Battalion. It was expected that when he returned he would be able to offer an intelligence picture of British movements. Discovering two German servicewomen operating the telephone switchboard, Bittrich asked them to repeat every piece of information they received to his headquarters – a promise they kept, earning themselves an Iron

Cross apiece. He decided not to wait for Kussin but drove back to Doetinchem.

After an hour at his headquarters, there was still no news. In darkness, he drove back towards Arnhem, finding Harzer's command post among the woods by Staadsbosch. One battle group, he was told, had been sent along the railway towards Wolfheze under the artillery commander, Lieutenant-Colonel Spindler. Another was moving south towards the Rhine between Arnhem and Oosterbeek; a third to Arnhem road bridge, which various sources reported as captured by the British on the north side. Harzer's operations were not made easier by the fact that there were a number of small units or detachments fighting in the area who were not under his command. Hence they passed their information back to other headquarters and much of what he had received from them had been on a chance basis.

Bittrich decided that nothing of what he had heard or seen necessitated a change of plan. He needed only to refine his arrangements. All the remaining units of 10th SS Panzer were to leave at once for Nijmegen, taking the ferry at Pannerden to avoid delay in fighting the British at Arnhem bridge. Harzer would get his reconnaissance battalion back from Nijmegen but should meantime use the reconnaissance unit of the 10th. He was at once to assume command of all units in Arnhem and Oosterbeek. Operations by 9th SS Panzer were to accomplish three tasks:

'1. To break the resistance of the British forces at the Arnhem bridge and to recapture the north end of the bridge.

2. To prevent the movement of reinforcements to the British forces at the bridge from the landing zones at Oosterbeek.

3. To reduce the enemy sector as soon as the additional troops and armour (which has been requested from Army Group B) arrive in the area and, having reduced the sector, to destroy the troops inside it.'

Spindler's battle group had already struck the 1st Battalion near the railway. Obliged to move without one company which failed to find the rendezvous, Dobie's column made a

Brigadier Lathbury commanded the British 1st Parachute Brigade

painful journey across country through the rain and darkness. He noted in his diary:

'0300 (Monday). Very bad going through woods with guns, carriers etc. Bumped enemy post X tracks 697797 approx – caused enemy casualties – enemy withdrew. Major Bune and mortar detachment missing.

0430. Reached road junction 709783 – S Company ran into enemy fire – Enemy armoured cars off road – MG fire, 20 mm. and mortars. Attacked with S Company left flank – gained northern enemy position and inflicted casualties.

0700. Passed HQ Company 3rd Bn – took them along . . . '

The 3rd Battalion had by morning been cut in two by Harzer's battle group working south towards the Rhine bank. Quite apart from the weakness of the two halves, Brigadier Lathbury's jeep and radio were now separated from him. While he was considering what his best course would be, a liaison officer from divisional headquarters appeared under the guidance of a member of the Dutch resistance. Urquhart and Lathbury were told that the second lift with the 4th Parachute Brigade and glider reinforcements were expected at 1500 hours. The two men decided to break away from Fitch's column to return to their headquarters.

'Would you care to throw a bomb, sir?' asked the brigadier, offering his divisional commander a smoke grenade.

'No, you're much better at it than I am.'

The smoke burst in the open and Urquhart, Lathbury and his Intelligence Officer ran out into the street. Captain Cleminson of the 3rd Battalion, watching their departure, saw that they were making in the confusion of the moment directly towards the Saint Elizabeth Hospital which he knew to be occupied by Germans. He dashed after them but a machine gun fired quickly, nicking Lathbury's spine. He was paralysed. The three officers lifted him into a house, 135 Alexander Straat, occupied by a middle-aged couple who offered their front room.

While they examined the brigadier and wondered what they should do

Brigadier 'Pip' Hicks.

now that he was injured, a German soldier's face appeared at the window. Urquhart quickly raised his automatic pistol and fired, killing him. A few moments later, the householders, who had withdrawn to converse together, came back to say that they would hide the wounded man and look after him. It was a generous act; they would both be shot if the Germans discovered what they were doing. Carrying Lathbury to a cupboard under the stairs, the three officers left by a side door and continued their journey.

At the bridge, Frost and his force remained in possession of the northern end. One company and the 2nd Battalion headquarters had reached it on the previous evening just as the Germans began to take up positions at the southern side. The railway bridge had been blown up in the faces of C Company as they seized it; B Company had attacked and screened the column from the knoll of Den Brink as they passed and A Company had completely killed or captured the remaining fifty enemy attempting to obstruct them, the field security police from II SS Panzer Korps. Later, brigade headquarters under the brigade major had arrived. Part of the brigade's company of parachute engineers swelled the garrison and, after daylight on the Monday, inspected the bridge to find that it contained no

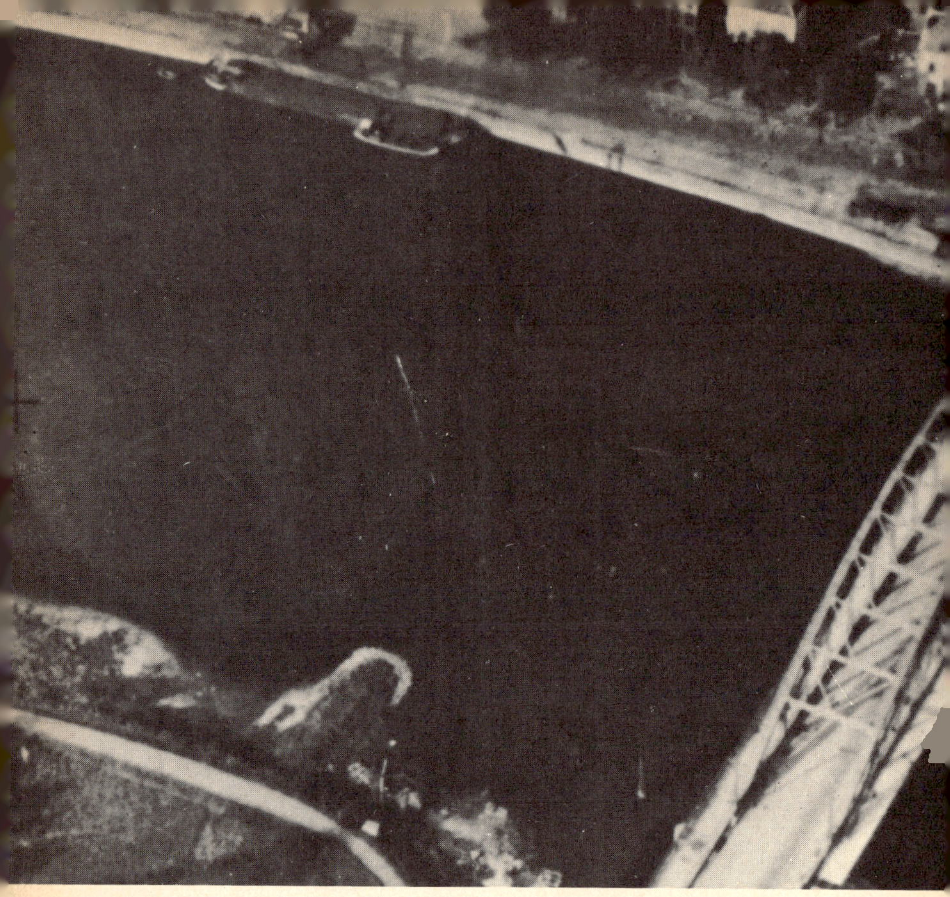

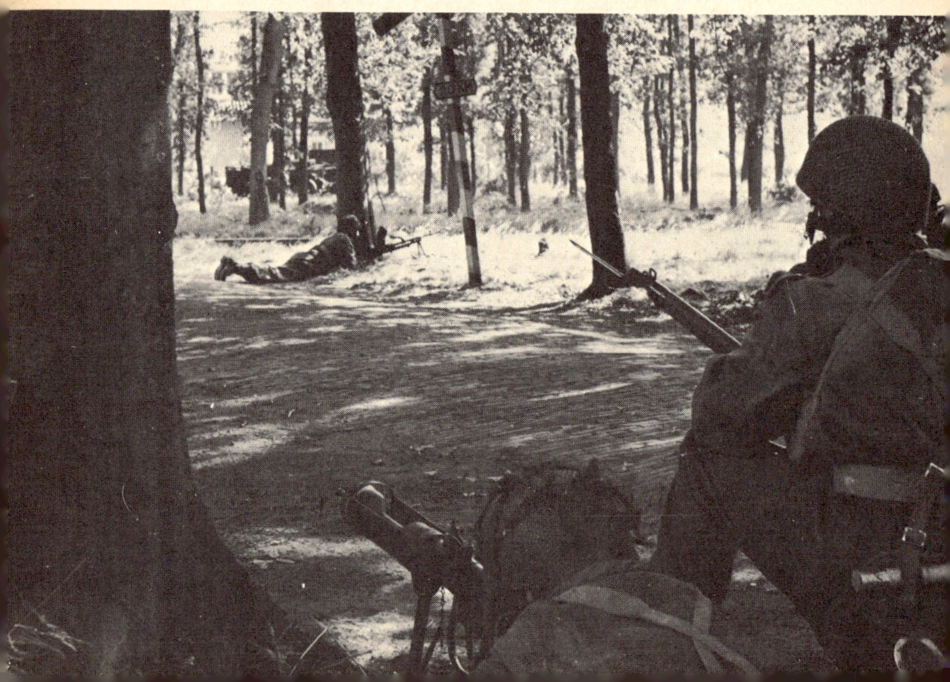

Above: Arnhem road bridge. *Left:* British paratroops in the woods near Wolfheze. The man in foreground is holding a Piat gun

demolition charges. This and other news was relayed to divisional headquarters through the artillery wireless net of the Forward Observation Officer. It was a comfort to know that the guns of one battery were close enough to support them.

Two gallant attempts were made to capture the southern end of the bridge but the enemy had mounted 20mm flak guns to fire directly down the long open roadway. The Germans attacked from both ends at various times but failed to dislodge the parachutists. Returning from Nijmegen, Harzer's reconnaissance battalion attempted to force their way across from the south and succeeded only in leaving ten of their vehicles blazing on the elevated paving under the grimly satisfied eyes of the defence.

Between these attacks, there were almost continuous battle noises from the town. Dobie had brought the 1st Battalion close to Den Brink and the Saint Elizabeth Hospital but the attacks they had made to reach this point had left him with only eighty-two unwounded men. The fit could no longer carry the casualties and the trail of their dead lay back through the streets held by *Kampfgruppe* Harzer. The 3rd Battalion were in an equal plight. The several commanders in the area were hoping increasingly that the arrival of the second lift from England would bring some relief.

At divisional headquarters, General Urquhart had still not returned: Brigadier Hicks of the Air-Landing Brigade had therefore assumed command. During the Sunday and the Monday morning, the battalion and half battalion which had arrived with

121

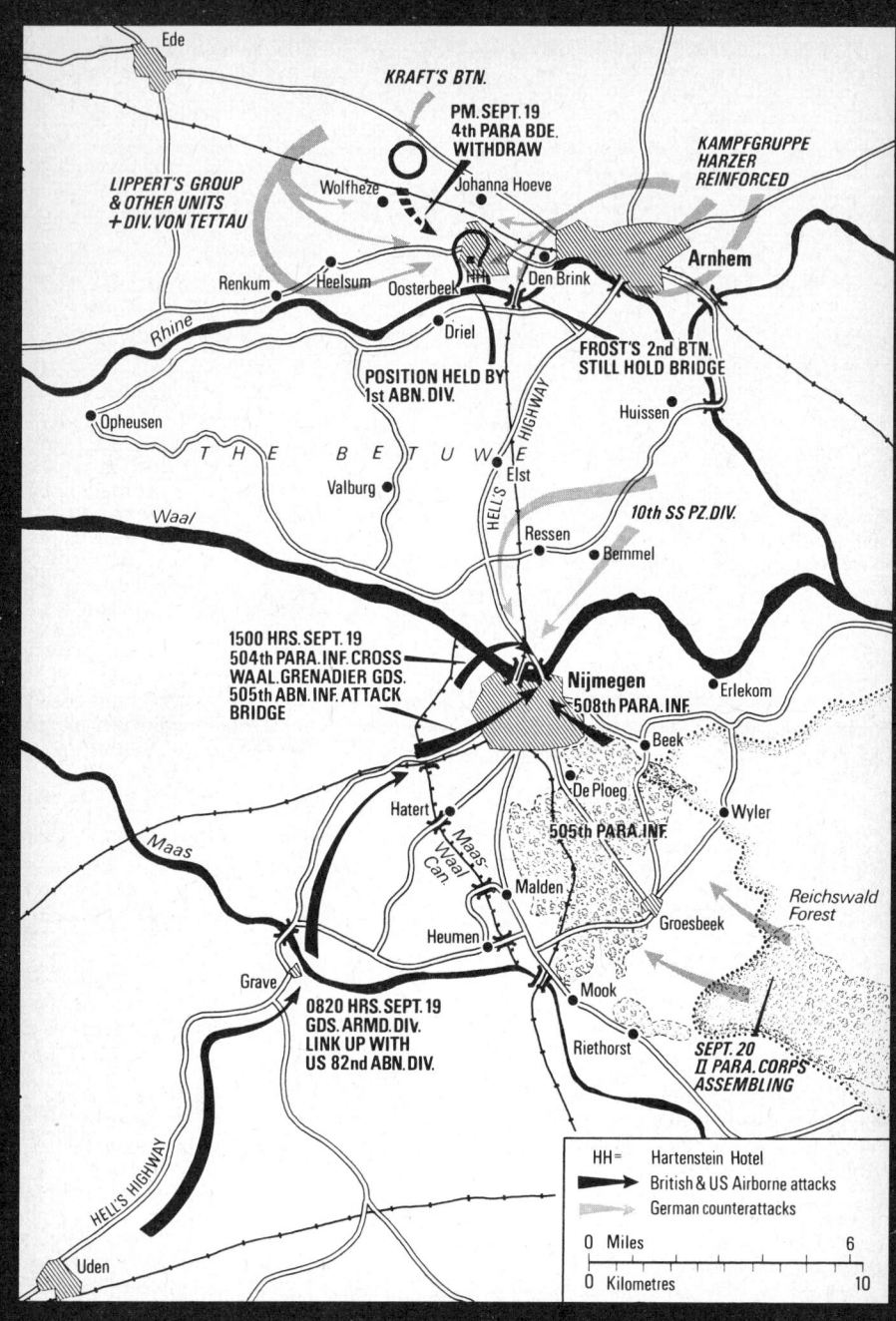

The situation in the US 82nd and British 6th Airborne Divisions' areas on 19th/20th September

him by glider had been holding the dropping and landing zones to be used by the second lift. The attacks against them by Tettau's units had not been worrying, though the zones were too expansive to be sealed completely against infiltration. The needs of Frost's force, as reported by the artillery, were more serious. At 0945 hours, the half battalion of glider infantry were ordered to make their way to the road bridge and inform the brigade headquarters, incidentally, that all the radio frequencies had been changed in an attempt to improve communications. The glider battalion remaining, 7th King's Own Scottish Borderers, stretched out their line of posts to repel infiltrators.

It had been planned to fly in the second lift during the morning but the weather did not permit it. It was 1500 hours before the aircraft appeared and the enemy had now full details of their direction of flight. Christiansen had moved a number of flak batteries into position while Tettau's division made a special effort to attack with Colonel Lippert's Herman Göring training units, a police battalion and the Dutch SS under Helle. Amongst them were other 20mm flak guns. The price of restricting air transport operations to a single sortie per day, with or without the loss of the operations plan to Student, had now to be paid at Arnhem as it was being paid by Gavin at Nijmegen and Taylor in the south. In one of the 4th Brigade's aircraft ' . . . Suddenly we saw a couple of planes behind us go down and somebody said, "There go some poor buggers" . . . Then we heard steel hitting the bottom of the plane but thank God nothing came through.' Some distance away, Captain Frank King of the 10th Battalion noticed 'many anti-aircraft guns and of course at 500 feet we were vulnerable even to MG and rifle fire . . . The American crew-chief was killed near the door. There was a certain disorder but no panic . . . I gave the order to jump . . . both plane engines were blazing.'

There was not only much more flak; the parachutists and glider units were landing on zones under aimed small arms fire and intermittent bursts from the flak guns, although the Scottish Borderers had successfully cleared or captured over 270 Germans from the immediate area. Brigadier Hackett, commander of 4th Brigade, did not of course know what had occurred to embarrass their reception but was vexed because in descending he had dropped his walking stick. Searching through the heather, he came on ten enemy soldiers to whom he called sharply in his excellent German, 'Wait here! I'll attend to you presently.' Finding his stick, he then marched his captives to the rendezvous appointed for brigade headquarters.

Awaiting him, he found Lieutenant-Colonel Charles Mackenzie, Urquhart's chief of staff, who told him all that had happened. Hackett did not like what he heard and resented the removal, without reference to him, of the 11th Battalion which was being sent directly to Arnhem bridge straight from the dropping zone without time to prepare for movement and independent of all other movements into the town. Senior to Hicks, he felt that the arrangements being made were not likely to restore control of the battle but, after some high words with his colleague that evening at divisional headquarters, the two men agreed a plan for the rest of the 4th Brigade within an overall divisional concept. With the 10th and 156th Battalions, plus the Scottish Borderers under command, Hackett would attack in the morning directly towards the high ground north of the city, taking the road north of the railway via Johanna Hoeve. They now had three brigades on the ground and had received a useful supply drop that afternoon. Unaware of the reinforcements journeying towards Bittrich, they were able to hope for a day of progress rather than desperate defence. Every day that they survived also brought nearer the prospect of union with the forces approaching from the south.

That night, at dusk, the Guards reached the southern outskirts of Eindhoven. Pausing only to shake the hands of their comrades in the 506th Parachute Infantry, they drove on to Zon. Within an hour of their arrival, the Royal Engineers were working to bridge La Prade's gap with a structure for tanks to pass over.

123

The struggle for Hell's Highway

Through Monday night, the field engineers of 14 Field Squadron worked without a rest to install their Bailey panels, girders and planking. By dawn on the Tuesday morning, their work was done and tanks of the Grenadier Guards group began to cross at 0615 hours. Two hours later, they were thirty-two miles on, greeting the 82nd at Grave bridge. The route across the Maas and the Maas-Waal canal into Nijmegen lay open. At Arnhem, only ten miles beyond Nijmegen, Frost's force hung on under attacks of increasing pressure. The corridor seized and held so efficiently by the 101st and 82nd seemed to have accelerated XXX Corps armour towards a close but successful race to their objectives beyond the Rhine.

So it might have seemed by a glance at the map. As in all life, appearance and reality are rarely the same.

Nijmegen bridge remained in German possession. On the south side, 10th SS Panzer had installed eleven towed or self-propelled 88mm anti-tank guns. The flak 88mm and 20mm guns had been reinforced in the open ground south again from these where they commanded the streets concentrating as radii towards a traffic roundabout by Huner Park. Overlooking this open expanse was the medieval tower of Belvedere, surrounded by enduring walls. Anti-tank and flak detachments around and inside the stout relic, across the park and on the northern bank were linked by the machine gun posts of Panzer Grenadiers who had drawn in all that remained of the original city garrison to strengthen the position. It was a formidable network of weapons.

The bridge was not the only factor inhibiting the advance. To the south, General Taylor still lacked the artillery he needed to cover his long area of responsibility and there was a recrudescence of the attacks against Hell's Highway.

Near the Best bridge, the faithful Wierzbowski's patrol hung on with extraordinary bravery. In the mist after dawn, the Germans attacked again, killing a number of wounded lying blind or unconscious. Private

Fighting for Hell's Highway – the end of an action

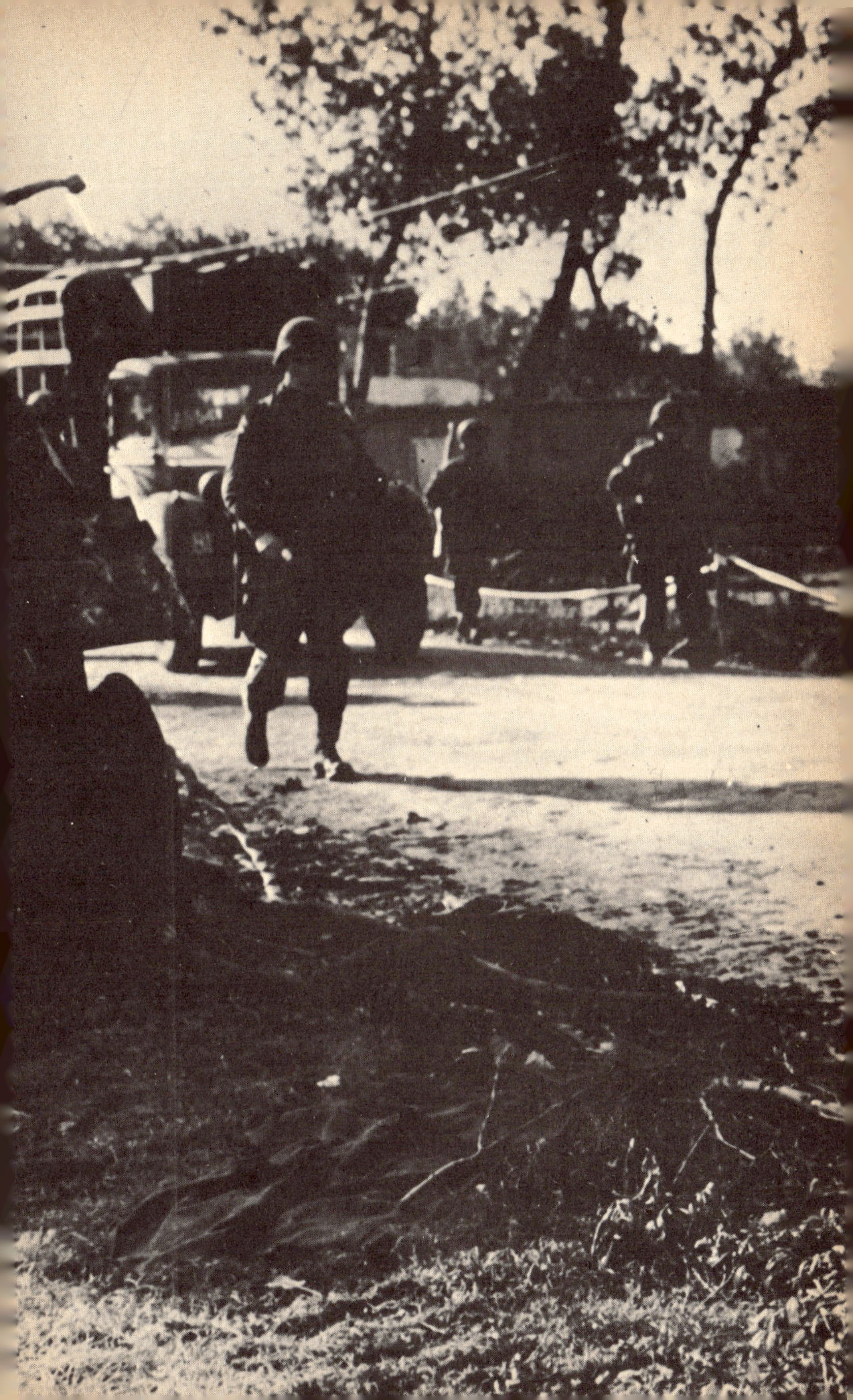

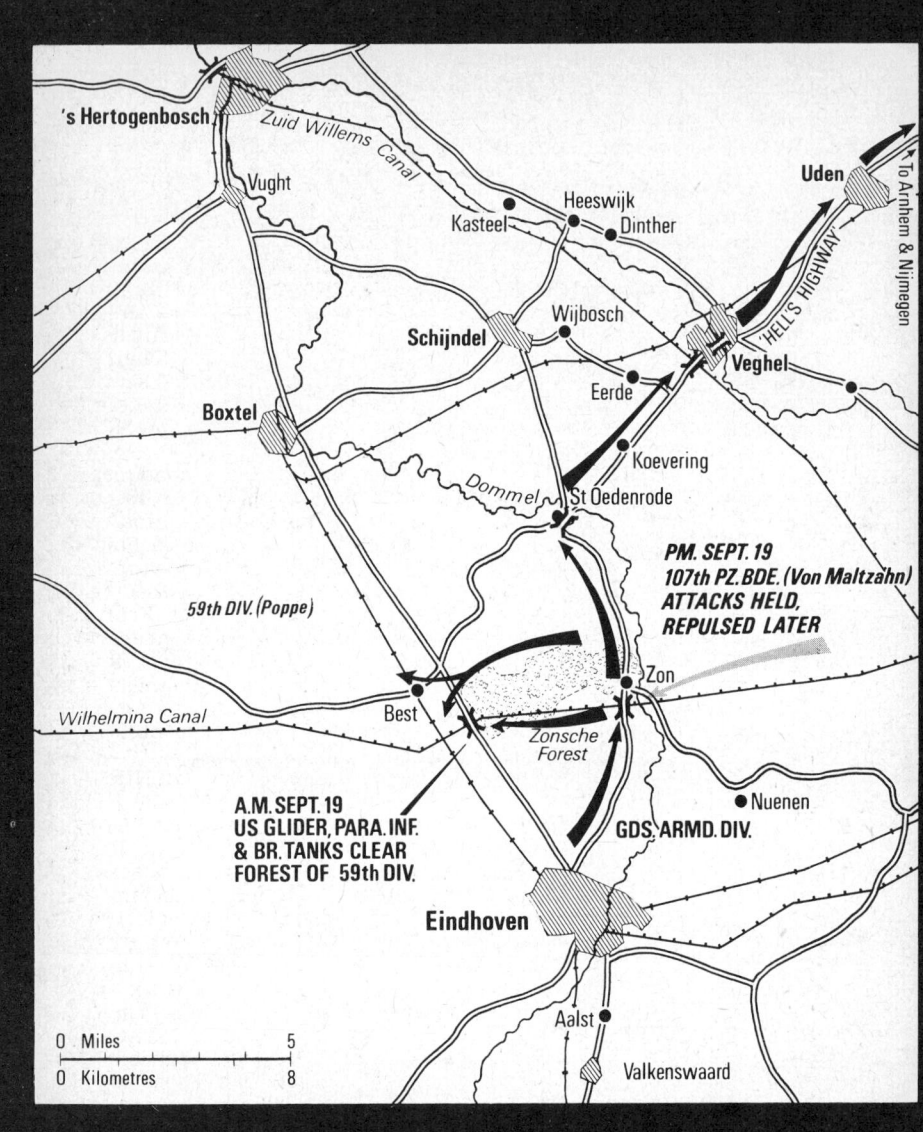

The situation in the 101st Airborne Division's area on 19th September

Joe E Mann with both arms stricken saved those remaining by throwing his body on to a grenade which dropped amongst them. When the enemy formed up to assault, Wierzbowski had only three men unwounded. Heavyhearted, he told one to tie his grubby handkerchief to a rifle and waved this surrender signal.

The two battalions nearby survived only because their combined strength defied annihilation, though the worst of their casualties on Monday night and Tuesday morning came from General Poppe's artillery. By midday, they were assured of a chance to retaliate. General Taylor sent a squadron of British tanks – the 15th/19th Hussars – and artillery assigned to him by XXX Corps to join his deputy, Brigadier-General Gerald J Higgins. With part of the glider infantry, the two parachute battalions already in defence and his British supporters, Higgins devised and commanded a counterattack which pressed and then began to encircle the Germans during the afternoon. The fire and counter-fire spread, intensified then suddenly dropped. As many as could of Poppe's 59th Division fled, leaving over 300 dead and 1,400 prisoners, a measure of their original strength around Best and the Zonsche forest. Lieutenant Wierzbowski and his tiny band emerged alive and free, having overpowered their captors in the final stages of the battle. At Oedenrode, Colonel Patrick Cassidy's battalion defeated a massed attack on his position.

Yet even as these local triumphs, these easements of the pressure from the west became known, an onslaught developed from the east. The 107th Panzer Brigade had arrived from Aachen under Major von Maltzahn – a little too late to strike simultaneously with Poppe's division and sever Hell's Highway but in time nonetheless to attack when all resources were committeed elsewhere. The Zon Bailey bridge had part of an American company, some British engineers and a tank troop to defend it besides General Taylor's headquarters. Maltzahn's Panther tanks knocked out the British armour and stood back to cover with fire from their guns the assault of their infantry. Divisional headquarters sent an urgent report to General Taylor that the defences were crumbling. Picking up part of the British 44th Royal Tanks, all that remained of the glider infantry and a 57mm anti-tank gun, the general returned to lead this force into a counterattack. The British armour opened fire at close range in the dusk. The anti-tank gun and the infantry's rocket launchers, aimed in the light of a burning British tank, hit several of the enemy half-tracks. Their dash was mistaken for numerical strength. Believing that a powerful counterattack threatened, the Panzer Brigade withdrew.

Further south, Corps headquarters had also had to join with tanks to reopen Hell's Highway. Behind them, a British division fought to hold the crossings of the Meuse-Escaut canal as transport columns crossed under enemy shell and mortar fire. From this starting point of the venture, and north along the single road, British supply trucks were burnt and broken by enemy action. The 'Indian raids' General Taylor had expected were developing.

General Gavin's plans at Nijmegen were partly dependent on the British transport columns. During the day, he had discussed with Generals Browning and Horrocks his plan to seize the bridge. One force of tanks and infantry should close in on Huner Park through the city while two parachute battalions should cross the Waal by boat and work up the north bank to the bridge's end. To do this, the 82nd needed British armoured and artillery support in the city and British boats for the crossing. Both these were at once promised but the boats could not be brought up Hell's Highway before the morning of the 20th. Impatient of delay, Gavin launched Colonel Vandervoort's 2nd Battalion of the 505th that afternoon with tanks and infantry of the Grenadier Guards. Under supporting fire from the guns of the 82nd and Guards Division the attack began at 1500 hours.

Why so late, we may ask all these years afterwards: with Arnhem so tenuously held, so urgently needing relief? Here is the difference between theory and practice. The orders have to be passed from the divisional com-

Above: German prisoners taken near Zon. *Far right:* An American paratrooper races through a field raked by 88's

mander to the soldiers who must fight. However efficient the staffs at the connected headquarters, there is a limit to the speed at which plans and orders, developing in detail at every level, can be transmitted. They must be checked against error – every timing, every map reference, every target for fire. Even when all this is done, the tanks and infantry must move to their final areas of assembly. Three hours passed between Gavin's orders and Vandervoort's attack with the Grenadiers. It was a competent preparation.

They approached the bridge from east and south. Soon the barrier of German weapons was in action, the streets shaken by explosions, misted by the dust of powdered masonry. The smaller element coming up from the south fought to a point 500 yards from the railway bridge but were obliged to halt when all their leading tanks were out of action. From the east, the assault force were in sight of the traffic roundabout when the fire from Huner Park became overwhelming. The infantry tried to force a way on by blowing 'mouseholes' through the walls of the intermediate building blocks. At the edge of the park they found the buildings fortified by the Germans and prisoners taken were discovered to be Waffen-SS of the 10th SS Panzer Division.

The discovery of the enemy's identity explained much to Gavin and the two corps commanders. It endorsed the need for a weighty concentric attack.

Unfortunately, the poor weather prevailed and the glider infantry, so urgently needed by the 82nd, did not arrive. Attacks were developing from the Reichswald forest sufficient to threaten the platoon and company posts on the approaches to the Groesbeek ridge; Gavin dared not remove any men from this sector. As a calculated risk, he reduced the bridge garrisons on Hell's Highway to produce all but two companies of Colonel Tucker's 504th Parachute Infantry for the Waal crossing. Two tank squadrons of the Irish Guards took up positions on the south bank to support the infantry; guns and Typhoons made ready to suppress the enemy on the north bank of this wide, deep and swift river.

The attacks on Hell's Highway had delayed the arrival of the boats and reduced their number from thirty-three to twenty-six. At 1500 hours, having had no chance to practise embarkation or paddling, the 504th began to board, loading down the flimsy wood and canvas craft with their bodies, weapons and ammunition. Encouraged by the gun and aircraft fire above them, the first wave cast off.

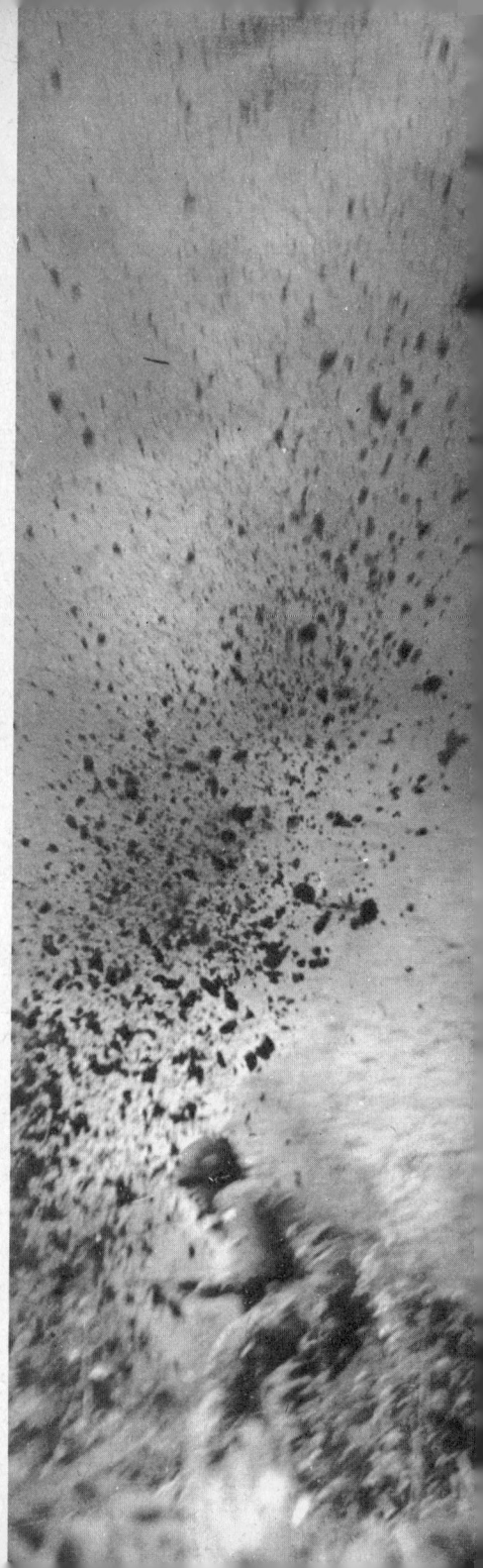

There was no cover on either side of the river and a sudden increase of speed and direction in the wind blew away the smoke laid by the gunners. German shell-fire dropped amongst them, exploding in the water, bursting in the air above their heads. Several boats nearing the northern bank were holed by machine gun fire and sank. Men were wounded, sank and drowned. Men were killed. But courage and quick wits saved some otherwise doomed. Captain Kappel of H Company threw off his equipment to dive after a drowning soldier. Private Joseph Jedlicka, submerged in eight feet of water, managed to hold his breath while he struggled up the slope to the north bank. Jumbled, disorganised but steadfast, the paratroops of the 504th scaled the nearby *bund* as the British engineers brought back the remaining boats to cross again.

Those first ashore stormed the enemy in their trenches along the dykes. Fortuitously, they were not members of the 10th SS Panzer or any first-class organisation. A bridgehead 750 yards across, 100 deep was taken. But as the movement along the north bank grew, after 1800 hours the quality of resistance hardened. What bore the advance along was the initiative and individual spirit of the many small groups, which penetrated every weak point of the German positions and refused to be pinned down by fire. If one group could not get forward, others called that they would go round. The gunner observation officers called steadily for fire and the Irish Guards, spotting the progress by eye, fired their main armament again and again.

At last, Captain Kappel's company, mixed with I Company, reached the end of the road bridge. A few minutes earlier they had raised an American flag on the railway crossing to show that it was taken. On the south, the 5th Guards Brigade and Colonel Vandervoort's battalion had fought across Huner Park to the road bridge. Seeing the flag just after 1900 hours, Sergeant Robinson of the Grenadiers dashed forward with his troop. The bridge trembled with explosions. The Guards lost two tanks almost at once but the others mounted and crushed the 88s which fired the shots while at point blank range. Skidding, lurching, firing, sweating the two tanks reached the far side in a dead-heat with the leading squad of the 504th.

The bridge was theirs.

The road and rail bridges at Nijmegen were fully prepared for demolition before they were attacked. When Market began, Field-Marshal Model ordered their preservation,

Nijmegen. British Cromwell tanks cross the bridge

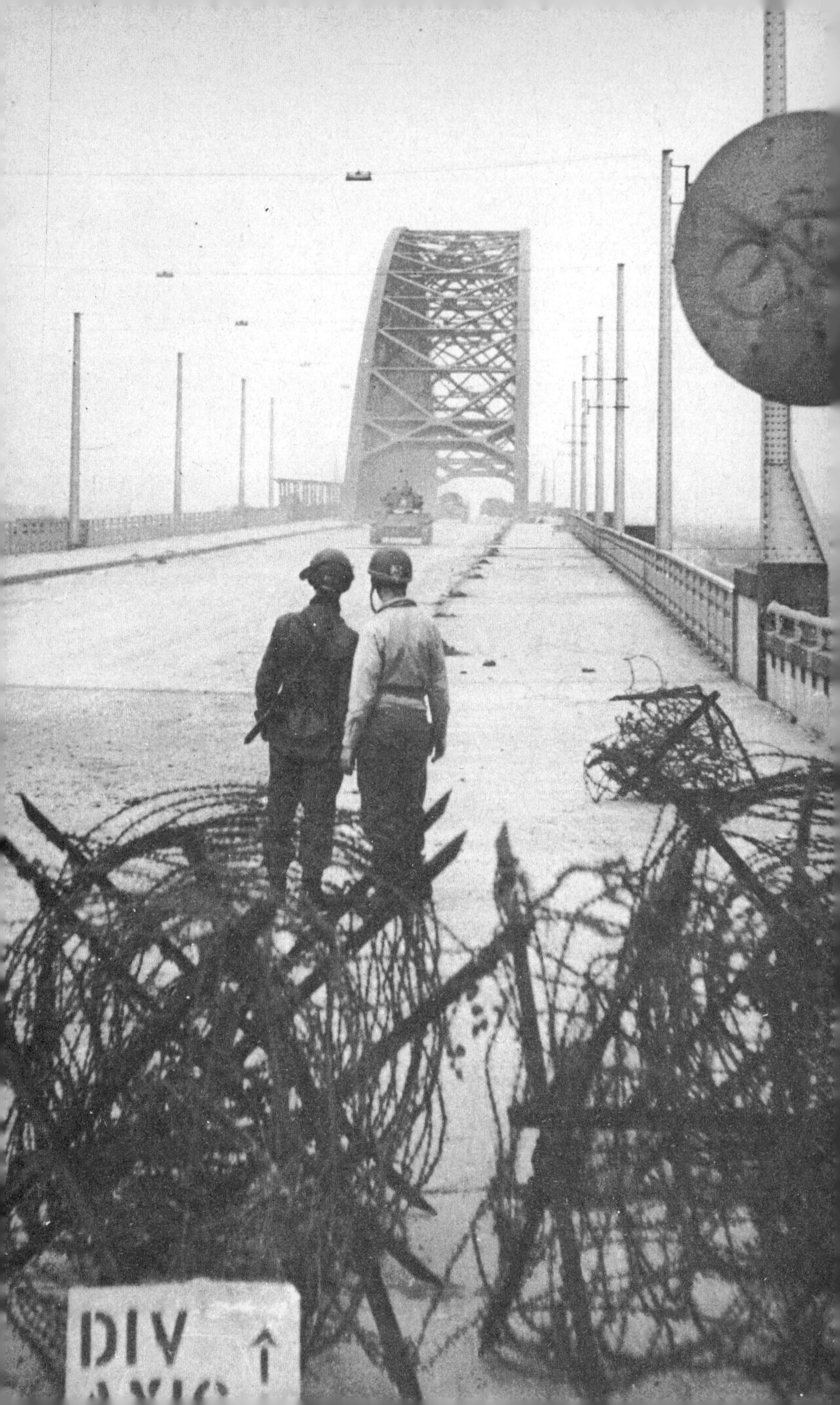
DIV

Above: Engineers remove the charges from Nijmegen bridge. *Below:* Relief from the Nijmegen action. *Right:* After the attack by the 9th SS Panzers

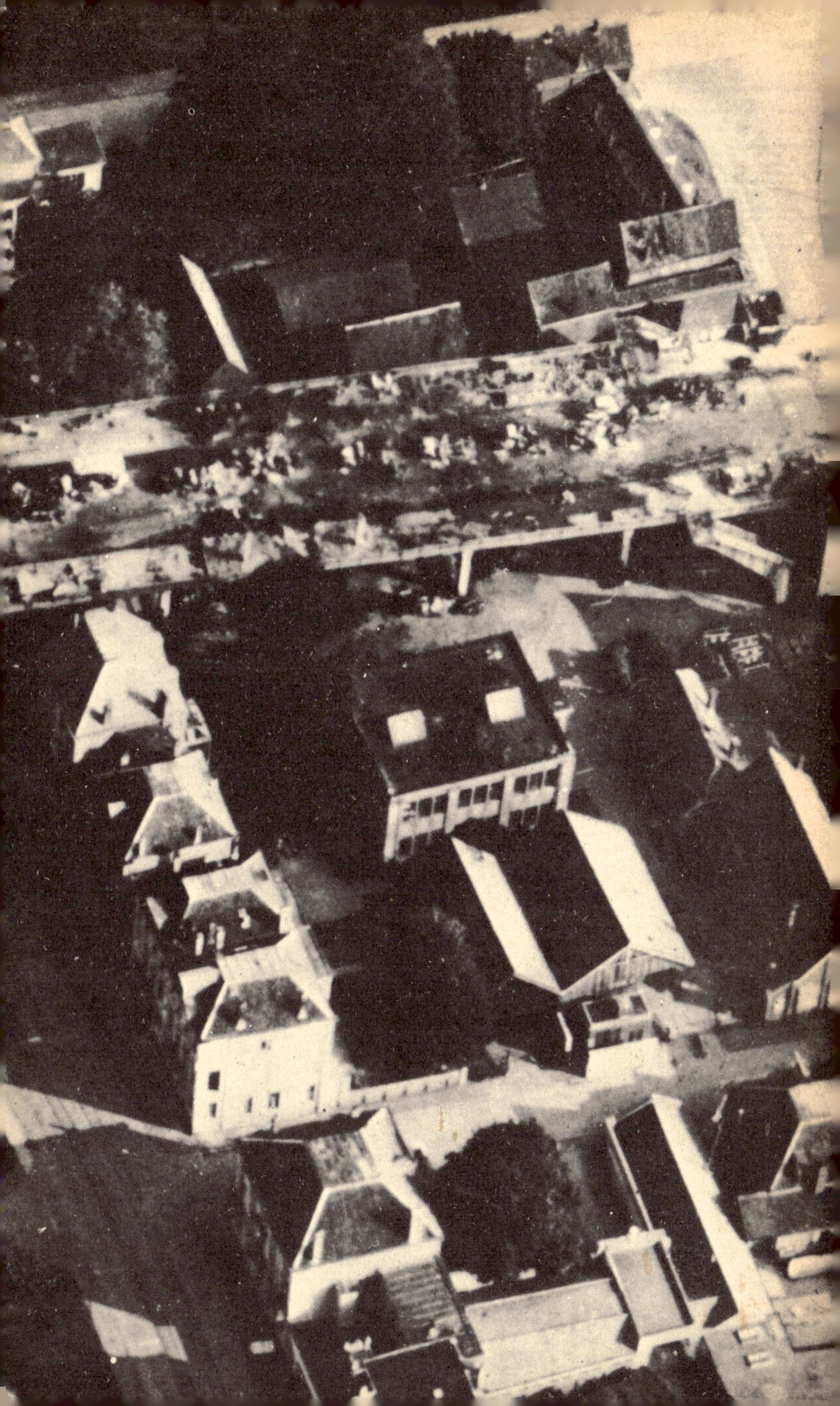

20mm Flakvierling
A quadruple version of the standard light German anti-aircraft gun mounted on a Half-track for greater mobility, especially in difficult conditions. Used against aircraft and also with telling effect against men and lightly armoured vehicles
Ceiling: nearly 20,000 feet *Rate of fire:* 700/800 rounds per minute per gun

believing that he had sufficient strength to hold the crossing places. In the last hour, a zealous subordinate might have ordered the firing of the charges, but were the circuits free? Captain Adams, released from the post office, believed his patrol had smashed them. A member of the Dutch resistance had independently cut cables he believed to run to the charges. A British engineer officer descended to the chambers under the bridge and pulled the fuses out from the explosive just after Sergeant Robinson and the tanks passed overhead.

Whatever the truth of the matter, German reinforcements were unable to get to Nijmegen in time because of the British parachutists on Arnhem bridge. But this barrier, so stubbornly held, could not indefinitely withstand the reinforced strength of *Kampfgruppe* Harzer, urged on by Bittrich, pressed by Model to complete their destruction. The defensive posts were mostly in houses on and at each side of the earth ramp raising the road to the high bridge spans. Early on Tuesday morning,

'. . . a bit after stand-to [the dawn stand to arms] we heard engine noises from up the river. I looked out half expecting to see boats, but it was tanks and some SPs [guns] lumbering along the eastern road and bank. They didn't come too close – just stayed off about 1,000 yards and started taking pot shots – sniping, really, with bloody great cannon.'

These tactics were effective cover for infiltration by German infantry who worked their way towards the houses being slowly but steadily smashed. Often, the British paratroops were obliged temporarily to evacuate one or another group of houses under fire and the Germans took them by default. But as they were such an essential part of the bridgehead, they had to be retaken. Though the parachutists never failed to take back what they needed in the defence, each counterattack produced more stretchers with more wounded bodies for the cellars of the brigade dressing station, where the Royal Army Medical Corps doctors and orderlies had little rest. Almost every hour, too, the Catholic chaplain, Father Denis Egan,

75mm Pack Howitzer
Weight: 1,340 lbs *Rate of fire:* Six rounds per minute *Range:* 9,475 yards max

spent with dying men who did not think to ask, as he did not seek to assert what branch of the church he represented. When men are dying, faith is a much simpler problem.

Men and ammunition were what Frost needed to hold on. He was still obtaining devoted support from Major Mumford's battery of 75mm guns near Oosterbeek but, shells being short, the gunners were only asked to help repel major attacks. Anti-tank ammunition was reduced to about twelve rounds of 6-pounder and seventeen for the infantry projectors at midday.

There was no sign of the 2nd South Staffords or the 11th Battalion; no news of the surviving elements of the 1st and 3rd Battalions. In the afternoon, a number of houses shelled frequently through the morning began to burn beyond control. At dusk, to add to their concern, what appeared to be a fresh squadron of tanks appeared on the north west edge of their perimeter. All approaches were now occupied by German armour as well as infantry and assault guns.

On the Tuesday morning, Urquhart got back to his headquarters at 0725 hours. For over twelve hours, he had been forced to hide in an attic and was only relieved when the 11th Battalion and the remainder of the South Staffords reached his house. Borrowing a jeep, he drove back to find Mackenzie in one of Model's former hotels in Hartenstein.

'We had assumed, sir,' said Mackenzie, 'that you had gone for good.'

A report was made to him concerning events in his absence and Hicks returned to his brigade.

Urquhart was now seized of the necessity to appoint a commander in Arnhem to control the drive by the 11th, South Staffords and the 1st and 3rd, if they could be found, to join Frost at the bridge. Hopefully, since he had himself returned unscathed, he sent off Hick's deputy, Colonel Hilary Barlow, with a staff officer, a radio and a jeep.

Through the morning, reports came in from the staff visiting the Air-Landing and 4th Brigades and from the gunner net working to the bridge. The actual position of most units became accurately plotted. Less accurate was the information concerning

Above left: Lieutenant-Colonel David Dobie. *Above right:* Major Freddie Gough.
Below: Brigadier J W Hackett

Above left: Lieutenant-Colonel Eddie Myers. *Above right:* Major Dickie Lonsdale.
Below: Captain Lionel Queripel, VC

the enemy because, although over 1,800 prisoners had been captured, so many units of such strange origins had been identified. It was known, however, that the attacks against the 1st Borderers and a party of glider pilots from the west and north were being run by Colonel Lippert whose NCOs school and training battalion was assisted by sailors, airmen and a mixed bag of soldiers with anti-aircraft guns in support. Helle's Dutch SS had also been identified but their prime aim was self-preservation. There were therefore gaps in the enemy line, particularly to the north, and through these a reconnaissance troop of Gough's squadron searched and questioned. One message of many from the Dutch was that one hundred fresh tanks had arrived that day, Tuesday, the 19th, from Germany.

This report reached divisional headquarters at 1155 hours. If it was true, the division would be able to continue operations only in a very limited area. Contact with Second Army to the south at 1015 hours had told them that the Guards Armoured Division were at Grave and the bridge at Nijmegen had yet to be taken. Urquhart began to think that he must stop the 4th Brigade and close his division into a single perimeter.

About 1330 hours on the Tuesday afternoon, he found Brigadier Hackett by the railway east of Wolfheze station. As the two men met they were strafed by three Me 109s, whose attacks at Arnhem were made possible by the low and heavy cloud over Belgium and Britain.

'Unless the enemy alters his plans in such a way as to favour us,' said the brigadier, 'there's not much future for the brigade on its present line of advance.' A change was unlikely; he was right up against a cordon established by Major Spindler, who had four additional units under command, including Krafft's battalion. The heaviest strike weapon of the parachutists was the 75mm howitzer, and the little shells of these weapons merely rattled against the German armour.

Warning Hackett to be ready to pull back and then try the middle road into Arnhem – the Heelsum-Arnhem road – General Urquhart went back to his headquarters. He had not been gone more than thirty minutes when a message came to the 4th Brigade that an enemy force (Lippert's, with armoured cars and self-propelled flak guns) had worked round to the south of the Air-Landing Brigade and were moving towards Wolfheze and the railway. All the 4th Brigade Transport and anti-tank guns were north of the track. If Wolfheze station and crossing was captured there could be no disengagement to the south. The brigade commander ordered the 10th Battalion to come back to hold the area while he disengaged the remainder.

All this took time. The 10th reported: 'The battalion was in close contact with the enemy and [withdrawal] meant moving back across about 1,000 yards of open ground which was swept by small arms. It had to be carried out, however, and the companies got back to the level crossing at Wolfheze. Very heavy casualties were suffered crossing the open ground...'

Captain Lionel Queripel, commanding a company of the 10th, was concerned to keep men moving; for as soon as the withdrawal was observed by Krafft's men and the neighbouring battalion, they fired every weapon to hand and called their mortars and guns into action. With his own face laid open by shrapnel, Queripel carried a wounded sergeant to the safety of a ditch, and then rallied a few men to join him in an attack on the nearest enemy post from which two MG 34s were firing. A British 6-pounder was also held by the Germans at this point and the little party killed the enemy crew on it. The machine gunners fled. From the flank, a section of Germans began to work their way back to the machine guns, throwing stick grenades to cover their movement. Captain Queripel received another face wound and was shot in the arm.

Now in a German trench, the party took shelter. 'Get out,' said Queripel to his party, and remained to throw grenades while they withdrew. Looking back, after a dash of one hundred yards, two of the soldiers saw that he was still fighting when the enemy rushed in, killing him where he stood.

Withdrawal in war is never an easy movement. When fire breaks up the ranks, even the best regiments are liable to disorder, perhaps a momentary panic. The dreadful movement back under fire became a nightmare as, suddenly, gliders bringing in transport and anti-tank guns of the Polish Brigade began to land amongst them and receive their share of German missiles. The pilots had found the right landing zone but the division believed it had cancelled their passage. Behind, RAF transports flew in to drop supplies into the hands of the enemy. One, captained by Flight-Lieutenant David Lord of 271 squadron was seriously damaged by flak. Like so many of his colleagues, he flew steadily on with his task despite an engine beginning to catch fire. The crew were ordered to jump to safety. Then, even as the flames spread, he returned alone to make a second run so as to release the last load of bundles, when his Dakota crashed, a fiery mass, to the ground.

At dawn on Wednesday, as the 82nd and the Guards made ready finally to capture Nijmegen bridge, 1st Airborne Division was being crushed out of existence.

On the Wednesday morning at the bridge, Colonel Frost found himself '... lying face downwards on the ground with a fiendish pain in both legs', after what seemed "the hell of an explosion".' He had been seriously wounded by a mortar bomb and Major Freddie Gough now took command of the defences.

It became clear as the morning passed that the bridge was slipping from their grasp. The German infantry were kept back from it, were forced out of the houses through which they sought to break through to the ramp and northern span, but the armour grew hourly more bold as the tank commanders sensed progressively that the British anti-tank weapons were almost extinct. Presently, two Pzkw IIIs, painted a buff yellow, drove up to the ramp on the western side, paused and traversed their guns a little. Then two more appeared at the end of the ramp, up which they drove until they were level with the first span and looked down into the houses by the river bank. Covering one another,

Panzer-Grenadiers attack houses by the Rhine

Above: Harzer's armour. *Far Right:* The British supplies drop wide

each crew watched to see whether any would pay a penalty for this deliberate approach, so close to the defended houses, so much in the open. Apart from a few grenades thrown from windows, there was none. Almost at leisure then, the tanks began a slow destructive fire into the buildings, using a variety of shells – solid steel, high explosive and white phosphorus smoke, the latter hastening the process of burning out these nests of resistance. Panzer Grenadiers began to advance in little rushes through the gardens on the western side, closing towards the houses immediately below the bridge.

The German tanks and infantry were also co-operating a mile downstream between the Rhine Pavilion and the Saint Elizabeth Hospital but less effectively. Here the area was not so open. Harzer's armour lacked a ramp from which to fire down directly into the paratroops. In consequence, his infantry and engineers were committed to the meticulous and deadly work of fighting house by house, aided at times by fire from the artillery positioned in the brickworks on the south bank. It was these guns which had fired decisively on the previous day when the 1st and 3rd Battalions, the 11th and South Staffords had sought to break through to the bridge. In this attempt, 272 officers and men had been killed or wounded, among them all four commanding officers. Colonel Hilary Barlow, sent by Urquhart on the Tuesday morning to command the four battalions, had been struck down on his journey to them. He remains missing to this day. What was now left in the area of the Rhine Pavilion and between the roads running parallel with the river bank was a threadbare defence, much of it unconnected, the men weak for want of rest, confused by the action continuing blindly hour by hour. Lieutenant-Colonel 'Sheriff' Thompson, the artillery battalion commander, returning from one of his frequent visits to the accessible defences drew together as many as he could and reported to General Urquhart on his return that a single commander and a wireless set were urgently needed in the area.

There were few experienced commanders to hand, fewer still unwounded. In the dressing station, however, was Major Lonsdale, second-in-command of the 11th Battalion who had been wounded while still descending under his parachute. Patched up, he had been asking for discharge and a task. Urquhart now gave him one with orders to take a radio offered by the gunners and to assume command of the sector on the river bank towards the bridge. Arriving intact, Lonsdale made a quick tour of his force and saw that their hold was a tenuous one: the South Staffords had withdrawn to the Oosterbeek church in rear and what remained (he noted) was '... throughout that afternoon mercilessly bombed and attacked by the Hun. Later that afternoon, German flamethrowers were used to great effect in that they set fire to the nearby woods and with the wind in the wrong direction for us, the smoke and flames made our position uninhabitable. As a result, I spoke to Div. HQ on the wireless, informing them . . .

Arnhem bridge

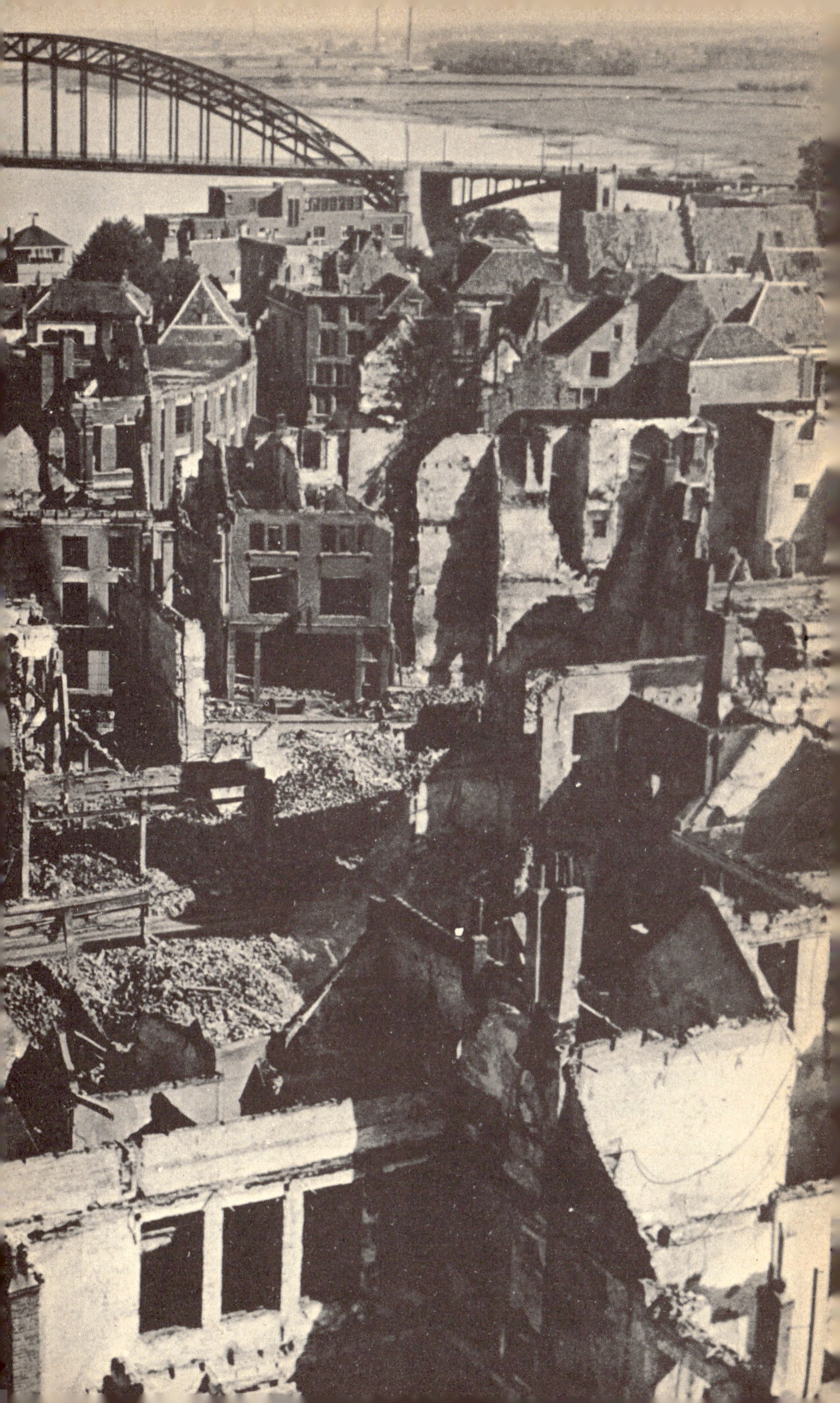

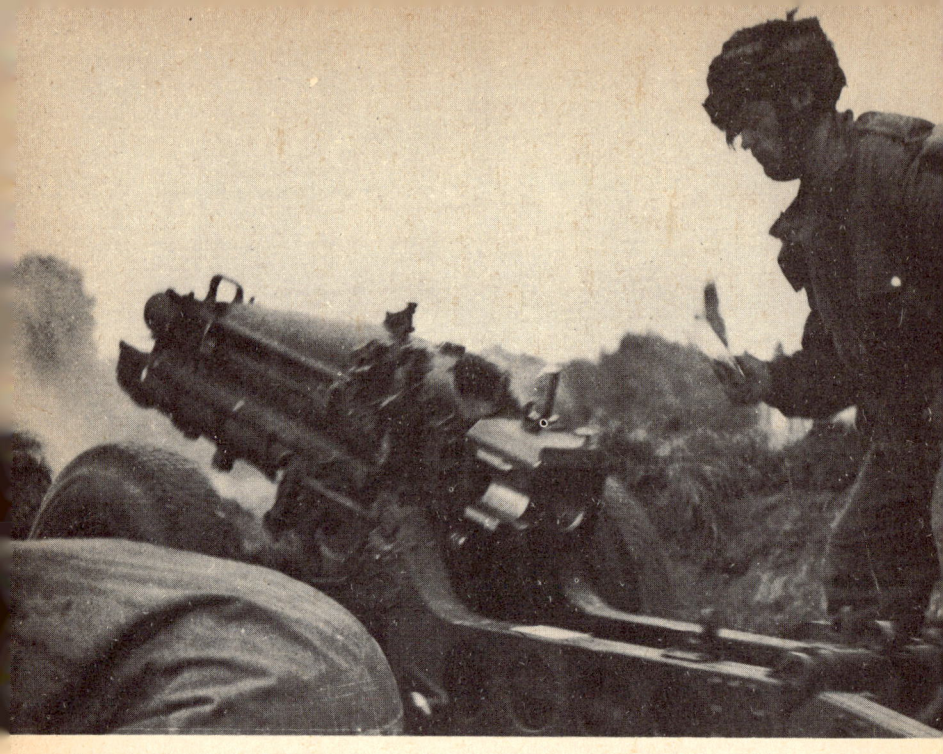

Above: **The guns remain in action.** *Below:* **A medical orderly kneels at the grave of a fallen comrade**

that I would like permission to withdraw to the area of the church. The staff officer to whom I spoke replied: "The man on the spot must decide", to which I replied: "OK, in half an hour's time from now I am bloody well off to the church!"'

At 1845 hours, in the confusion of the smoke and an incipient German attack, Lonsdale's force made a dash back to the area of the church. It was a mixed body but now reorganised with gunners and glider pilots integrated with the infantry. One chaplain, Padre Watkins of the 1st, remained amongst the party, a true guide, comforter and friend. 'The padre got me out,' a soldier of Lonsdale's force wrote home to his parents, 'and a lot of others. I don't know why he didn't get hit, I didn't hear him saying any prayers.'

The new positions of Lonsdale Force constituted the eastern sector of a divisional defence perimeter. For now that he could no longer hope to relieve Frost with additional troops and supplies, General Urquhart had decided early on Wednesday morning simply to hold fast to a portion of the north bank to offer a bridgehead to XXX Corps when it came to the end of Hell's Highway. To the west and north, the perimeter was manned by Hick's Air-Landing Brigade, effectively about five companies; the resilient and enterprising pathfinder company; the reconnaissance squadron and various detachments – glider pilots, Poles who had come in by glider, gunners without guns, engineers without plant, administrative troops. Divisional headquarters remained in the hotel at Hartenstein. Thompson's 75mm batteries were spread out to fire in support of sections of the defence.

It was expected that the 4th Parachute Brigade would make an important contribution to the defence as soon as it could be brought in from the area south of the railway, but on the Wednesday morning it was still two miles from the remainder of the division. Brigadier Hackett had once again to disengage in daylight from an enemy stronger in numbers, mobile and armoured. Thanks to his cool head they accomplished this without disaster but it was not thereafter a straightforward matter of marching directly to the nearest divisional defence posts. The Germans were now closed round the division and the 4th Brigade were obliged to force a way through them; in effect, to run the gauntlet. The first intimation of what was happening to them came when a number of wild-eyed men rushed into divisional headquarters to be stopped by Urquhart and MacKenzie. They were from the 10th Battalion, a handful of survivors from an ordeal by fire. A little later, sixty more of the 10th marched in under their commanding officer, on his feet but mortally wounded. In the woods behind, Brigadier Hackett was leading by fieldcraft and bayonet assault all that remained of his formation, seven officers and seventy-eight men. In the defence line that evening, the 4th Brigade was a company strong.

When Brigadier Hackett reported to his divisional commander, it is not surprising that he asked at once for news of XXX Corps. It was what everyone wanted to know, what everyone discussed every hour: where were they; when would they arrive? Urquhart's headquarters had not yet made contact with either Horrocks' or Browning's staffs behind Nijmegen and they declined still to use the Electricity Board's private telephone circuit. Fortunately, an army liaison station and the BBC correspondent who had accompanied the glider force gave them occasional communication to London and increasingly through the day news of the attack on the bridge at Nijmegen. Just after 1400 hours, they heard that the Guards Armoured Division and 82nd were fighting hard for the Waal bridge. If they captured it that afternoon, men asked one another, was there a hope that they would reach the Rhine next day, Thursday? None doubted that the divisional perimeter would resist for some time, even though the bulk of their supply had again been dropped into German positions. But could the bridge defence be sustained for another day?

From the bridge came a report that Tiger tanks had arrived: four and a reconnaissance half track had passed across to the south that evening. The artillery observation post had been blown from its last eyrie and was

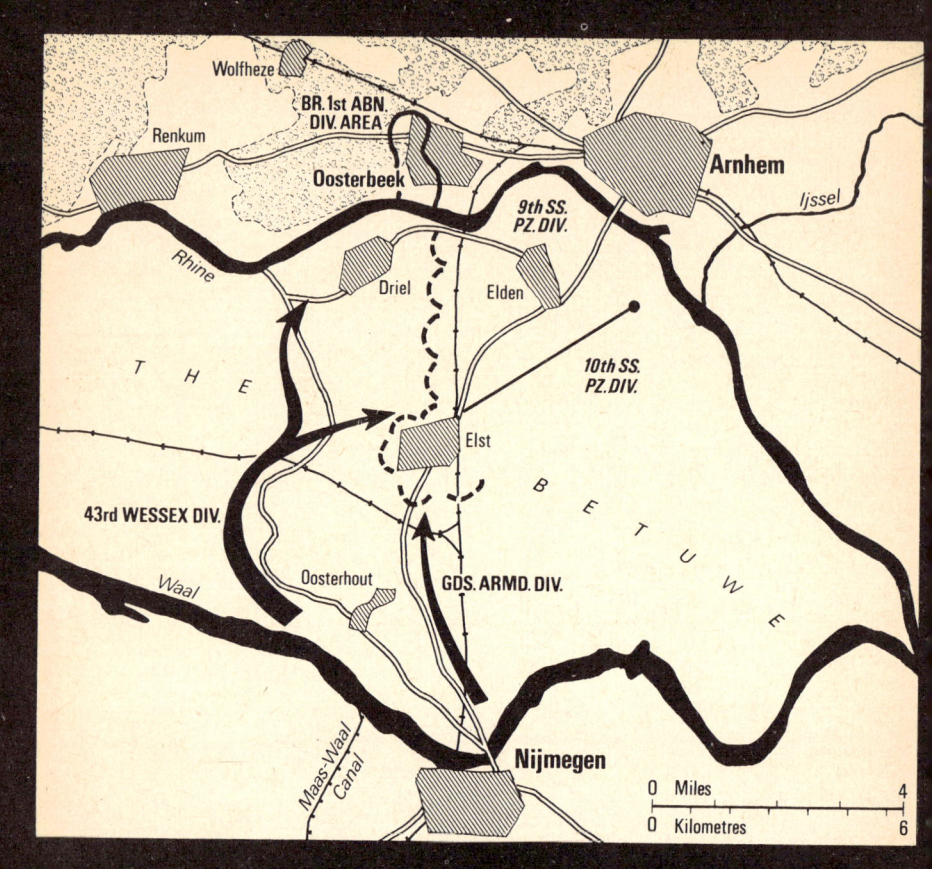

The land forces' drive north from Nijmegen to relieve the 1st Airborne Division

closed. All houses immediately west of the first span had been lost; smoke from others nearby was pouring into the cellars where the wounded lay and the doctors had told Freddie Gough that they would be asphyxiated if they remained there. A truce was arranged and the stretchers were carried out, many to the Saint Elizabeth Hospital where British doctors and staffs attended with the Dutch to friend and foe without discrimination, while German guards looked on. The truce was honourably observed by the Germans, though they did not hesitate at its conclusion to crowd in upon those remaining to fight. The battle began again; the night passed with a band of diehards still in position, denying to the Germans the use of the bridge by unarmoured vehicles.

Towards midnight, the firing died away everywhere, save for an occasional slow spasm of harassing fire by German guns. To the south, the night sky flickered, too, with the flashes of shells exchanged intermittently across the Waal. And at last, at midnight a message came from headquarters, Airborne Corps, to say that the Nijmegen bridge had been captured intact, that armour was passing across towards Arnhem.

Throughout the Tuesday and Wednesday, all the reinforcements Model had promised Bittrich were arriving in the Arnhem area: additional infantry – though much of this was suspect morally or physically – a training battalion of engineers with flame throwers, artillery of which the guns had to be towed into position by Harzer's own transport and, at the end, weightiest of all, the King Tiger tanks of *Abteilung 503*. All these were committed piecemeal as they arrived because Bittrich believed that his pressure at Arnhem was at the point of being overwhelming, that with each fresh reinforcement the British must crack.

He was mistaken. He had taken pains to reorganise the German forces to the west of Urquhart's perimeter so that Colonel Lippert commanded all the troops in that sector. If he had paused to mount a comprehensive attack, using Lippert's force as a backstop, while driving in with *Kampfgruppe* Harzer reinforced by the King Tigers and the engineers, Urquhart's defences must have been destroyed.

Model's refusal to have the bridge at Nijmegen blown added to Bittrich's difficulties; for with its capture, II SS Panzer Korps also began to fight under the pressure of time. If the Guards Armoured Division began to advance quickly between the Waal and the Rhine, he would have to divert forces from Arnhem to impede them and this would delay his destruction of the 1st Airborne Division. On the Wednesday night, he told Harzer that the last pocket at Arnhem bridge must without fail be pinched out on Thursday morning and a concerted effort be made during the day to finish off the larger sector resisting by Oosterbeek.

Events were running late for Army Group B as much to the south of Nijmegen as to the north of it. At headquarters, First Parachute Army, General Student was now aware that his plan to cut Hell's Highway by pincers west and east through Best and Zon had been thrown out of timing by the counterattacks of General Taylor's division, British armour and guns. He ordered a renewal of this operation. In the Reichswald forest, the advanced units of Meindl's II Parachute Korps were arriving from Germany but rather than wait for the whole to form up, he directed that an attack should be mounted at once, on the Wednesday morning against the Grossebeek heights. Thus Gavin's thin defences were pressed again just as the struggle for Nijmegen bridge demanded all available support in tanks, guns and infantry. Hell's Highway came again under shellfire and was blocked as before by burning vehicles.

When Thursday came, the British 43rd Wessex Division, the infantry needed to assist the Guards' tanks forward to the Rhine, were still struggling to get forward along the highway.

'Boys, it is all hell'

On Thursday morning, as soon as it was light, Major Brinkmann's SS battle group began to clear Arnhem bridge of his persistent foe.

While five Pzkw III tanks and an assault gun fired from several points of vantage into the upper storeys of the few houses still occupied by the British, Panzer Grenadiers worked methodically through the ground floors.

Initial entry was achieved by blowing a 'mousehole' and as soon as the explosive fired, stick and egg grenades were thrown inside. Protected by the outer wall, an assault team of three or four soldiers waited only for the shock of detonation before they too hurled themselves through the hole, spraying the room of entry with bullets from their Schmeisser machine pistols. In theory, this method was irresistible. In practice, it was inhibited by the British paratroops' preparations; they had constructed shelters of rubble and fallen beams in corners and alcoves, on stairways and in the entrances to cellars. When these were run down, '. . . one young Britisher began to dodge about to draw our fire, while another tried to come at us from the side with a knife.' 'One man remaining leaped at us swinging his rifle as a club.' As if these attempts were not hopeless enough, two of the tanks kept pace with the Panzer Grenadiers to fire directly from the street into the front doors or windows. At the last, a second group of Germans rushed the houses from the opposite end of the block to catch about forty paratroops attempting to withdraw through the gardens.

'Jimmy Logan (the medical officer) estimated that the 2nd Battalion wounded are 210', noted their diarist; that is, about half the battalion, a figure which excluded the dead. 'Ninety-four were rounded up on D plus 4 [Thursday]' and about a further fifty of brigade headquarters, gunners, engineers, signallers and Service Corps, of whom twenty-seven were wounded. The diehards had delayed the opening of the bridge for a further three hours and a half. By 0915 hours that morning, however, German trucks, in addition to armour, were passing over it freely

The wounded accumulate

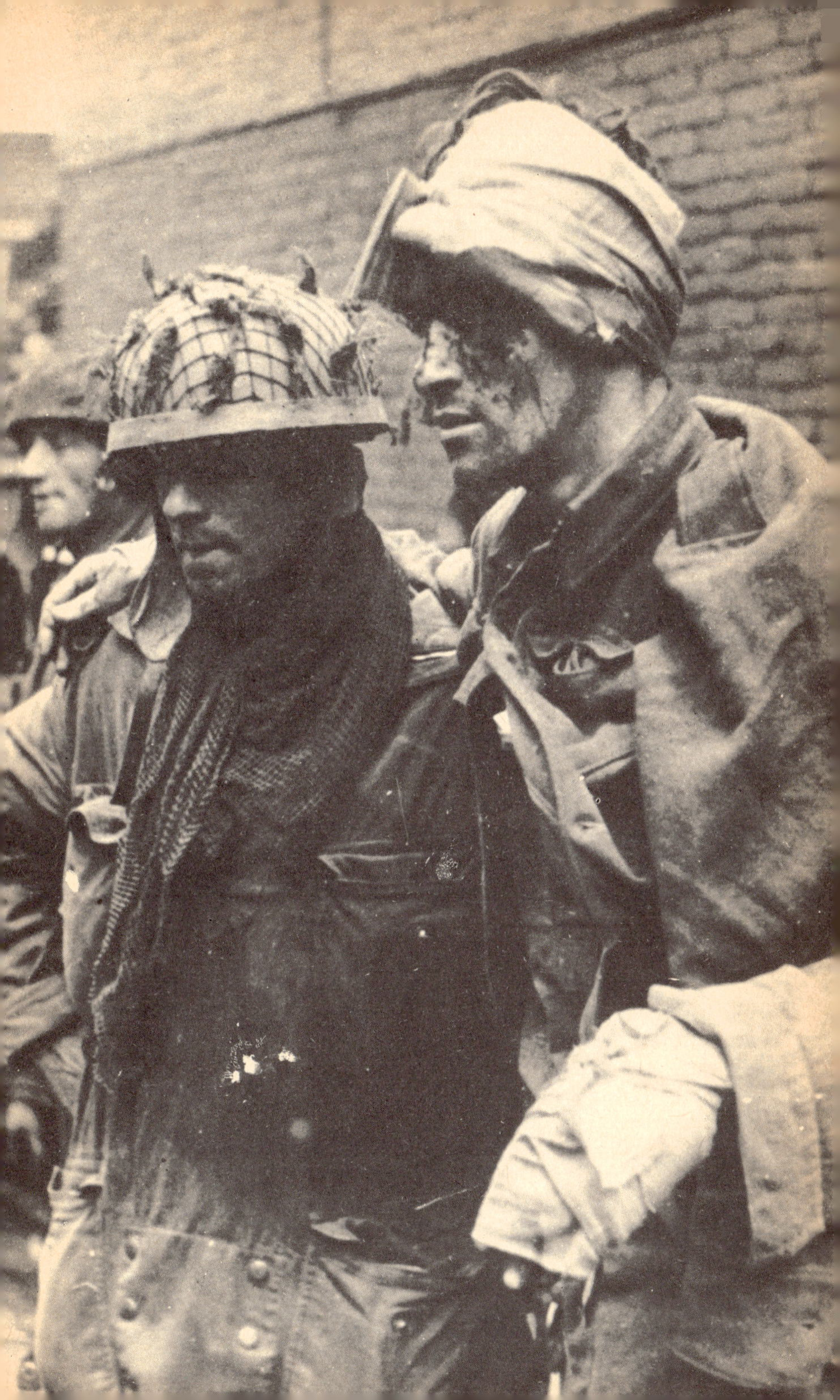

towards Nijmegen, into the Betuwe, the island between the streams of the Rhine and the Maas.

With the clearance of Arnhem bridge, the outcome of Market Garden became a simple issue: which side would gain the bridgehead held by Urquhart's men? North of the Rhine, the British were denying ground, the Germans attacking; to the south, the roles were reversed.

On the Thursday morning, the Guards Armoured Division sought to open a corridor through the Betuwe. They found themselves in an expanse of flat farmland, much of it intersected by drainage ditches and relieved only by the comfortable structures and tiled roofs, the gardens and orchards of the small towns, villages and farmsteads from which the paved roads ran at right angles. With few exceptions, these roads were built-up on solid banks to a height of six feet to carry them above the flood level. Now, on this late September morning as the mist cleared, they exposed the tanks perfectly to the gun-layers of the 88s deployed and concealed by 10th SS Panzer Division during the previous night. The Irish Guards Group came to a halt.

There are days in war when, from the first moment of action, a series of mistakes and mischances combine to frustrate success. So it was for the British in the Betuwe on the 21st September. Having halted, the Guards attempted to place tanks out to a flank to shoot forward of their infantry, advancing along the ditches on either side of the road. But below the road level, the sodden *polder* would not take the weight of the armour; the first troop to slither on to it became bogged. It was necessary to find a side road and this necessitated mine clearance. When at last the infantry were able to move forward, they were heavily mortared and because of the attacks on Hell's Highway, the British ration of shells and mortar bombs for the attack was small. The attack did not succeed in clearing more than a few hundred yards, past the first anti-tank post. Behind this, there were more 88s in depth, protected by machine guns and *panzerfaust* rocket launchers; behind again, tanks were seen.

The defences were not impregnable and the lack of supporting fire for the infantry might have been borne had the air force been able to strike as it had done on the march to Eindhoven. But this day, the RAF air contact team on the ground could not communicate with the Typhoons which circled overhead. The Germans were surprised and elated to see the Luftwaffe joining the fight with Me 110s and Fw 190s! At nightfall, the Guards had not advanced a mile beyond the bridge.

It was a dismal day, lightened only by three events for 1st Airborne. The first was that direct radio contact was made with the gunners of XXX Corps by an observation officer, Captain McMillan, of 1st Airborne Division. General Urquhart was making his morning round of visits to units when, about 0930 hours, he discovered his chief artilleryman, Colonel Loder-Symonds, engaged in a strange conversation by wireless.

'... Yes, and my Christian name is Robert....'

'What is your wife's name?' – a question from the distant station.

'Merlin.'

'What is your wife's favourite sport?'

'Falconry.'

This seemed enough to overcome the suspicions of the artillery radio station in XXX Corps that McMillan's call to them and Loder-Symonds' subsequent conversation were not part of a deceitful plot by German Intelligence to break into a British wireless network. In consequence, the weapon power of 1st Airborne was boosted – the guns of 64 Medium Regiment, eleven miles to the south, were now ranged and corrected on to German positions close to the perimeter. In time, more medium and some of the heavy batteries would be able to add their strength, to return to the Germans some of the weight of shells that they were throwing into the slender tongue of Dutch land held on the north bank.

Then, at 1800 hours that evening, the Polish Brigade arrived.

Each day, the Germans had feared the arrival of reinforcements by parachute. The air observation and early warning system had learned to

British vehicles devastated by German artillery and mortar fire

watch especially for the transport streams approaching the coast and to report their passing not only to the Luftwaffe fighter squadrons but also directly to the army at Arnhem. Already, this system had caused much loss and damage to the air supply crews. Those arriving at 1245 hours on the Thursday were severely attacked and little got down to the defence. At 1600 hours supply aircraft returned and managed to drop a number of little bundles and paniers inside the perimeter. While the anti-aircraft was concentrated upon them, Harzer received a message that 'four-motor' aircraft with gliders had passed over Dunkirk on the hour towards Arnhem. There were in addition three waves of Dakotas flying out of the dense low cloud over England. Reception arrangements were therefore made for General Sosabowski and his force. The waiting German soldiers at Arnhem noted that, '... the barrels of the anti-aircraft guns stared up into the sky from which there came to our ears a slight hum. It was the German fighters ... Suddenly the first anti-aircraft gun roared ... one after another, other batteries joined in the attack.'

Instructions had been relayed from 1st Airborne headquarters to the Poles that they should not drop on the *polder* south of the bridge but three miles to the south west, close to the village of Driel, whence they should seize the southern landing site of the Heavadorp river ferry. Delayed for two days by the persistent murk, tossed about during his flight through clouds, the fiery Sosabowski was in an angry mood when he reached his rendezvous, a condition made worse when he learned that half the aircraft carrying his men had failed to find the dropping zone. Undeterred, the Poles formed up quickly under random fire from German defences to work towards the ferry site. At this point, a woman member of the Dutch underground, Cora Baltussen, came to the headquarters to say that the Germans had attacked and captured the northern end of the crossing place, from which they were now firing directly across the river.

Unaware of these several setbacks to General Sosabowski's plans, General Bittrich believed that the entry of the Poles must be part of a fresh plan to link 1st Airborne with XXX Corps. He ordered Harzer to

151

Poles wait by the Rhine bank. They arrived too late

send a company of Pzkw V Panther tanks and Major Knaust's infantry battalion – newly arrived – to join 10th SS Panzer in their containment of the British at Nijmegen and to establish a blocking position south of Arnhem bridge against the Poles. These dispositions were particularly welcome to the 10th who would otherwise have been defending the whole of Betuwe. Now they might concentrate on the containment of XXX Corps. During Thursday night, Knaust's men passed south through Elst to find guides waiting for them in the dark countryside. Marched to their positions, they began to dig trenches amongst farm buildings and into the banks of the surrounding fields.

In the same darkness, Harzer brought across the bridge three other *ad hoc* battalions which had reached him, a machine gun battalion, Dutch SS *Landsturm* and a detachment of the King Tigers. These faced westward from Hell's Highway towards the Poles and sent patrols out to discover what Sosabowski and his men were about.

In darkness, Captain Zwolanski waded into the Rhine waters and swam across to the south bank. He was Sosabowski's liaison officer with General Urquhart. Admitted to the area by the Polish sentries he made his way to the farmhouse used now as brigade headquarters. Inside, his general was studying his maps.

Zwolanski was naked and dripping when he entered. 'What the hell?' asked Sosabowski.

'I have just swum across the Rhine to bring you the latest news, sir.'

'Yes, you look as if you have. Tell me what it is.'

During the day, Zwolanski reported, the Germans had attacked the Heavadorp ferry and then been driven back from it by the Kings Own Scottish Borderers. But the Germans returned and were believed to have a battalion sitting on the site. To get the Poles across the river, General Urquhart had ordered his engineer commander, Lieutenant-Colonel Myers, to construct rafts to ferry the Poles over. It was realised that this would be difficult and long drawn out but any strengthening of their numbers, particularly by fresh troops, would improve the chance of holding on.

Two companies of Poles made their way quietly to the river bank to wait. Elsewhere, the brigade captured a party of Germans sent out from

Hell's Highway and learned from them that an attack was to be made from this direction next morning. Sosabowski's own patrols reported that there was considerable enemy movement along Hell's Highway and a network of positions covering it from the west.

When dawn came on the 22nd, and there was no sign of the British rafts, the Polish commander drew in his two companies. With two depleted battalions to maintain his isolated position, he decided to close his ranks.

Early on Friday morning, the Household Cavalry once more combined audacity with skill to infiltrate part of a squadron through the mist to the Rhine. At Driel they found the Poles.

Back in the Nijmegen bridgehead, the infantry brought over the Waal on the previous afternoon did not make use of the morning mist to advance, as lamentably they had not been required to make use of darkness the previous night. At a comfortable hour, when they were once more able to see the ground ahead – and the Germans were able to see them, no less – the advance by 43rd (Wessex) Division began.

Whatever the reasons for this late start, the commanding officer of the leading battalion, Hugh Borrodaile, had no doubt that he must make haste. But in this flat miry land, he had no close air support, very limited artillery to help him on due to the interruption of shell supply along Hell's Highway, and no tanks to keep him company until he had rooted out the 88s opposing them. He decided to take what he could by infiltration. His rifle companies began to push along the ditches. When he came to Oosterhout village, however, this tactic was defeated; there was a 'battalion' – about 300 strong – defending it with a tank, several self-propelled and anti-aircraft guns and heavy mortars dug in amongst the houses. Colonel Borrodaile tried first one approach and then another using his own mortars and machine guns to support the riflemen and the fire of the single battery allotted to him. It would have been very surprising if these had succeeded and they did not.

His brigade commander, Brigadier H Essame, grew steadily more anxious as the hours passed outside Oosterhout. About midday, he saw that whatever the embargo, the Somersets needed full supporting fire. His forceful demands brought the divisional artillery on to the target.

While the Somersets made ready for a formal attack in full strength, Brigadier Essame concentrated a second battalion, the 5th Duke of Cornwall's Light Infantry with tanks and trucks, supporting machine guns and 17-pounder anti-tank guns to hasten through Oosterhout as soon as it was taken. The battalion commander, Lieutenant-Colonel George Taylor, was instructed to drive to the Rhine at Driel without a pause.

At 1520 hours, the Somersets' companies went forward. At 1700 hours, Oosterhout had been cleared out, 139 prisoners taken with a tank, an 88mm gun and five light flak guns. The remainder had managed to withdraw at the last minute. The confusion and speed of their flight was shortly to aid the Duke of Cornwall's Light Infantry.

Having placed himself directly beside Borrodaile, George Taylor knew at once when the road was clear. A bizarre figure in breeches, a parachutist's smock and a despatch rider's helmet, he leapt into his jeep and bade the column move with all speed. Round the village, through the smoke on the far side the column disappeared, many of the infantry dangerously exposed as they clung to the sides of tanks or crouched in open unarmoured three-ton trucks. The nearest Germans believed at first that this mixture of wheels and tracks hastening past from Oosterhout belonged to their own defence. They held their fire. But four miles to the rear, a detachment of SS in tanks and infantry grew suspicious and their commander moved them on to the road. Inadvertently, they broke into a gap in Colonel Taylor's column so that the chasers began to be chased. At dusk there was a clash. The Germans began to hunt for the intruders amongst the villages while the Cornishmen and their supporters laid ambushes with some success.

At Driel, Colonel Taylor drove into the village thirty minutes after leaving Oosterhout with his column.

Across the river, the slow progress of XXX Corps was understandably disappointing to Urquhart and his force. The general decided to send his chief of staff, Charles Mackenzie, and engineer commander, Eddy Myers, across the river to give his orders to the Poles and to impress upon Generals Browning and Horrocks that '... the Division no longer exists as such and that we are now merely a collection of individuals holding on. Make clear to them, Charles,' said General Urquhart, 'that we're terribly short of men, ammunition, food and medical supplies, and that we need some DUKWs [amphibious trucks] to ferry the Poles across. If supplies don't arrive tonight it may be too late.'

At 1210 hours, the two officers left divisional headquarters for the river bank where a rubber dinghy had been hidden. Mackenzie agreed to row, Myers to watch and he swore at his partner when he splashed his oars noisily. By luck, none of the German mortar or artillery posts saw them; the only fire was at long range from snipers and the bullets sizzled by at a distance. The little boat passed across and reached the high steep bank on the south side. In Sosabowski's headquarters, Mackenzie asked that every soldier that could be mustered should be sent across that night. They had been unable to make rafts but Myers had a suggestion: 'There are some small three-man rubber dinghies which can be pulled backwards and forwards across the river by hawsers.'

The arrival at Driel of the front half of George Taylor's column that night seemed to promise success. But as the tanks began to move in, two mines exploded beneath their tracks so that the remainder had to wait until a way forward was found for them. A more immediate setback was that the DUKWs brought by the battalion could not negotiate the steep river bank. They were obliged to rely therefore on the little dinghies and such rafts as they might improvise. After three hours, the dinghies began to ferry a few Poles at a time from a crossing held by the British light infantrymen. The rafts foundered; all but one of the dinghies became holed. Captain David Storrs of the engineers rowed and rowed hour after hour, making twenty-three crossings and by morning fifty Polish soldiers and perhaps a ton of ammunition and other supplies had been carried into the perimeter.

At 0915 hours in the drizzling rain on Saturday morning, General Urquhart sent this signal to Airborne Corps headquarters:

'Spasmodic shelling and mortaring during the night. Movement of self-propelled guns noted. Otherwise little change in the perimeter. Several attacks by infantry and self-propelled guns or tanks supported by extremely heavy mortaring and shelling are in progress on north east of perimeter...'

Yet another attack was being mounted. On the Thursday, Urquhart had subdivided the perimeter into a western sector under Brigadier Hicks, an eastern under Brigadier Hackett. Each had a number of units allotted by name for the defence – 1st Battalion The Border Regiment, or 21st Independent Company, or Lonsdale Force. But the terms, 'battalion', or 'company' were no longer meaningful; all units had become makeshift forces like Lonsdale's, and like Lonsdale's they were shrinking every hour as members of each force were killed or wounded.

The director of the airborne medical services, Colonel Graeme Warrack, could do little for the dying; his whole time and that of his exhausted medical officers and staffs was occupied with the treatment of those who had a chance of living. Sometimes, the wounded helped him in an unexpected way – Captain Frank King of the 10th Battalion lying on a stretcher saw a gravely wounded young soldier being sent away because there was no space for him in the crowded dressing station. He gave up his own place to the soldier and returned as best as he could to the battle. By Saturday, almost every wounded man who could move at all of his own accord had followed this example, yet the remainder continued to overflow.

With his divisional commander's permission, Warrack made his way to the nearest German hospital to ask the senior medical officer there for a safe passage to Harzer's headquarters. It was essential, if the lives of the

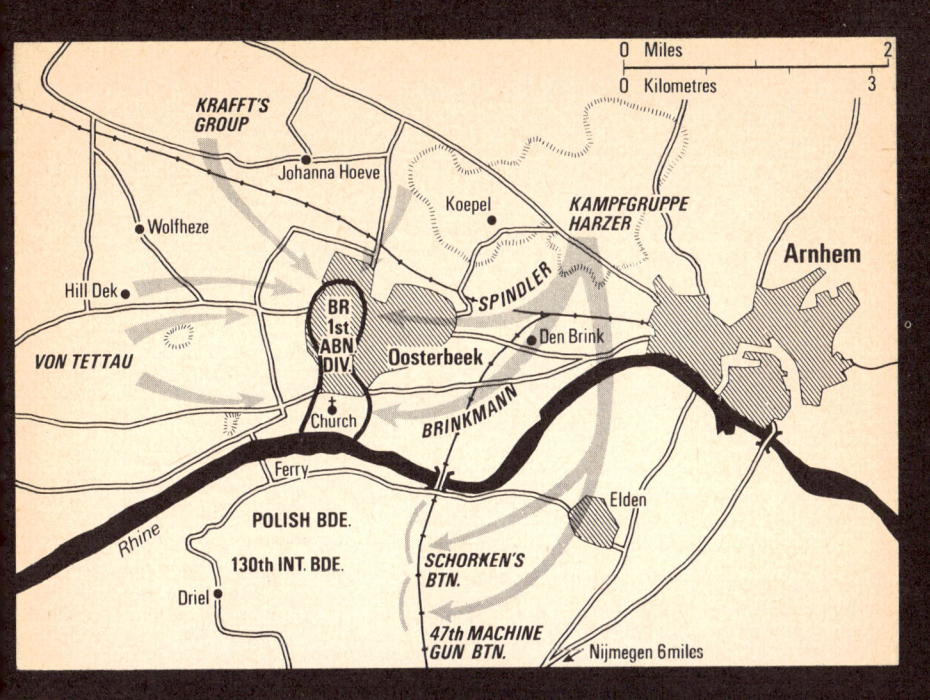

The position of the British 1st Airborne Division during its stand at Oosterbeek, when the Second Army arrived to relieve it

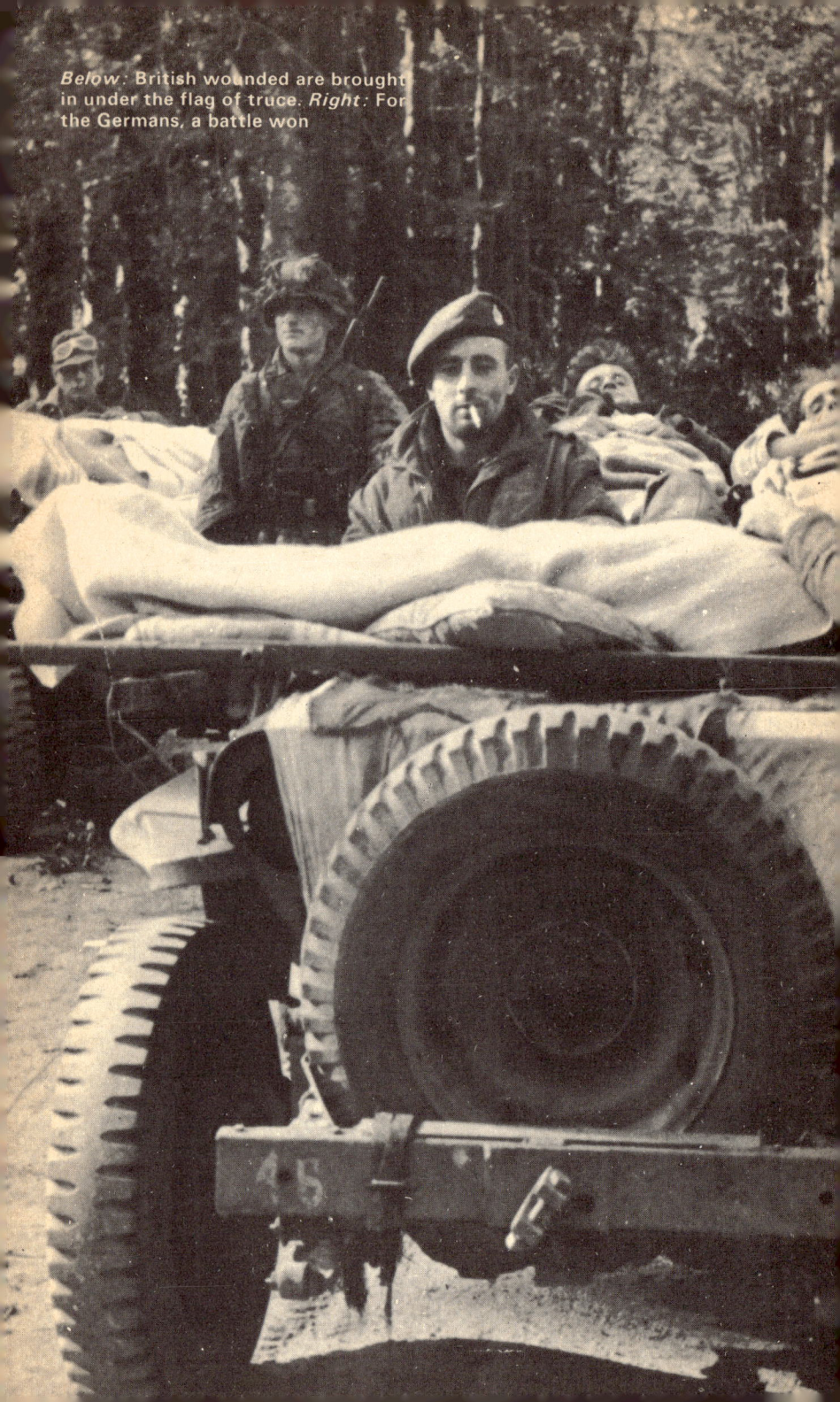

Below: British wounded are brought in under the flag of truce. *Right:* For the Germans, a battle won

seriously wounded were to be preserved, to arrange some form of evacuation with a truce.

Harzer's headquarters had moved from the woods by Staadsbosch into Arnhem city. As Warrack was talking to his chief of staff, Hauptmann Schwarz, Harzer joined them.

'I am extremely sorry,' he said, 'that there should be this fighting between our two countries. Of course, we will help you with your wounded men.'

A truce was arranged for two hours near the Tafelberg Hotel and on British jeeps, in German ambulances, 500 men were moved out of the immediate battle zone. As soon as they had gone, the fighting began again. At 1500 hours, a block of houses in the eastern sector was fired by the flame throwers of the *Panzerlehr* engineers. The heat from the blaze scorched a 'company' 200 yards away and burned to death at once those caught inside.

Saturday night was fine, the sky was clear and shining with starlight. At 2015 hours, Urquhart's situation report for the day read. 'Many attacks during the day by small parties infantry, self-propelled guns and tanks including flame throwers. Each attack accompanied by very heavy mortaring and shelling within Div. Perimeter. After many alarms and excursions the latter remains substantially unchanged, although very thinly held. Physical contact not yet made with those on south bank of river. Resupply a flop, small quantities of ammunition only gathered in. Still no food and all ranks extremely dirty owing to shortage of water. Morale still adequate but continued heavy mortaring and shelling is having obvious effects. We shall hold on. But at the same time hope for a brighter 24 hours ahead.'

Considering their circumstances, it was a moderate message. It was characterised by the cool fortitude which General Urquhart showed as he walked about amongst his units. 'His calm and cheerfulness,' remarked Marek Swiecicki, the Polish war correspondent, 'are really the sole cause of our optimism.'

By Sunday, though the general continued to preserve and encourage what remained of his division, all grounds for optimism had passed.

Three battalions of 43rd Division had reached the south bank of the river and one, the 5th Do sets, had begun a crossing on a few flimsy craft which drowned many of them. Such desperate devoted strategems were not enough at this late stage. There were only two practicable ways of relieving 1st Airborne Division: an assault crossing with a full complement of boats and bridges for tanks or an evacuation of the perimeter. On Sunday, General Student's final attack on Hell's Highway had closed it. Much of the engineers' boats and bridging were unable to come forward. Colonel Myers returned to his divisional commander early on Monday morning with letters. One was from General Thomas, commander of the 43rd Wessex Division. It told him that the idea of relieving and extending the airborne bridgehead had been abandoned. 1st Airborne was to withdraw across the south bank on a date to be agreed between Urquhart and himself. They would call it Operation 'Berlin'.

On Monday night, 25th September 1944, Operation Market Garden came to an end and Operation Berlin began.

It had been a dreadful day with frenzied attacks by the Germans. Snipers had begun to fire into some of the dressing stations in contrast to the otherwise generous attitude of the enemy to the British wounded. Tanks had driven into the gun lines and for a time the defence zone had been cut almost in two. Hungry, dazed for want of sleep, the airborne soldiers had continued to fight back doggedly, sometimes with wanton bravery. This saw them through the daylight hours until a wet blustering evening arrived.

As the fit and walking wounded made their way to the river, directed by glider pilot guides, their weary eyes saw everywhere strange shapes. The alarming spectres of the night were exalted by the groans of the dying and the stench of the dead.

Canadian and British engineers waited to ferry them across the river in light boats. XXX Corps artillery shot an accurate and devastating fire into the German lines. Late in the night, a corporal of the 3rd Battalion, a member of Lonsdale Force, climbed out of the little boat which had brought him over the Rhine and crossed the bank. He felt suddenly that he could not walk another step. Too tired to think of sleep, oppressed by the knowledge of the many friends he had left on the far side of the river, he could only repeat silently to himself, 'That's bloody that. That's bloody that!' until he was led to a truck which drove him away.

He was not quite right. That was not quite that. It was not all over so far as the struggle was concerned. On the far bank, already, the Dutch underground were combining with the British Special Air Service and members of the 1st Airborne Division to organise escapes. Major Anthony Deane-Drummond was to wait, standing in a cupboard, with extraordinary strength and patience for fourteen days until the Germans should leave the house in which he was hiding. Brigadier Hackett, now wounded, would be brought out and so would Brigadier Lathbury and a score in the dressing stations. After attending to their patients, Warrack and some of his medical staffs would escape.

The Dutch stayed on in their homeland, and they continued in secret ways to assist their allies, many to the extent of losing their lives, because they wanted their homeland to be free again. They had many months to wait.

The men of the 82nd and 101st, the men of 1st Airborne who came back and many of XXX Corps asked at first, 'Was it all a failure?' Seen so closely, it may have seemed such; and indeed so it seemed to some at a distance. Field-Marshal Smuts wrote to Mr Churchill from South Africa to sympathise for the setback. The British Prime Minister's reply provides, perhaps, an epitaph for the September battle: '. . As regards Arnhem, I think you have got the position a little out of focus. The battle was a decided victory, but the leading division, asking, quite rightly, for more, was given a stop. I have not been afflicted by any feeling of disappointment over this and I am glad our commanders are capable of running this kind of risk.'

Bibliography

The author gratefully acknowledges permission to reproduce passages from 'A Full Life' by Sir Brian Horrocks (Collins, London), from 'The Brereton Diaries' by L H Brereton, and from Mr Geoffrey Parson's article in the New York Herald Tribune. He also wishes to thank the executors of Mr Edward R Murrow's estate for permission to quote from his CBS News Broadcast

A Full Life Lieutenant-General Sir Brian Horrocks (Collins, London)
Airborne Warfare James M Gavin (Infantry Journal Press, Washington)
Arnhem Major-General R E Urquhart (Cassell, London)
Defeat in the West Milton Shulman (Secker & Warburg, London)
Freely I Served Stanislaw Sosabowski (Kimber, London)
Royal Air Force 1939–1945 H St G Saunders (HMSO, London)
The American Experience of War 1939–1945 K S Davis (Secker & Warburg, London)
The Army Air Forces in World War II W F Craven and J L Cate (University of Chicago Press, Chicago)
The Battle of Arnhem Cornelis Bauer (Hodder & Stoughton, London)
The Battle of Arnhem Christopher Hibbert (Batsford, London)
The Brereton Diaries Lieutenant-General Lewis H Brereton (Morrow, New York)
The Eighty-Five Days R W Thompson (Hutchinson, London)
The 43rd Wessex Division at War, 1944–45 Major-General H Essame (University of Chicago Press, Chicago)
The Guards Armoured Division Major-General G L Verney (Hutchinson, London)
The Rise and Fall of the Third Reich William L Shirer (Secker & Warburg, London)
The Second World War – 'Triumph and Tragedy' Winston S Churchill (Cassell, London)
The Second World War 1939–1945: Army – 'Airborne Forces' Lieutenant-Colonel T B H Otway (The War Office, London)
The Struggle for Europe Chester Wilmot (Collins, London)
The War 1939–1945 D Flower and J Reeves (Cassell, London)
United States Army in World War II: the European Theater of Operations – 'The Supreme Command' Forrest C Pogue (Historical Division, Department of the Army, Washington)
United States Army in World War II: the European Theater of Operations – 'The Siegfried Line Campaign' Charles B MacDonald (Historical Division Department of the Army, Washington)
We Defended Normandy Lieutenant-General Hans Speidel (Jenkins, London)
With Prejudice Lord Tedder (Cassell, London)
With the Red Devils at Arnhem M Święcicki (Max Love Publishing Co)